Tony Leck's
PAVILION ON A PLATE
Fresh Flavours From Guernsey

ACKNOWLEDGEMENTS

The idea has long been in my mind that, one day, I would put together a collection of recipes. Over the years I have supplied hundreds to various publications, be they local, national or international. So to me it seemed a simple matter of picking a few.

The reality was rather different, but here they are, a bookful of them… recipes selected for two reasons only. One, that you the reader will be able to cook the dishes at home. I don't hold with the chefs who choose to feature recipes that enable them to show off how clever they are. If you don't or won't eat it yourself then don't stick it on your menu.

Secondly, the finished result should be worth the effort of preparation. It should delight you with its taste and have you coming back for more. I hope my selection does that, and that you will enjoy using this book as well as reading it.

And so the acknowledgements. This is the bit that might get tedious for some, but hey… if you were part of it, this is YOUR moment and my thanks to you.

In no particular order… Martin Edwards for his belief, confidence and faith in producing said publication. Thanks to Paul Cocker for his unwavering enthusiasm… what would we do without email Paul?
To Carmel Stewart for her research.

To my close family Joanne, Georgie and Charlie for putting up with me while I threw my efforts into yet another project.

Thank you to Chefs Lawrence, Paul and others whom all taught me 'a thing or two'. To my mother, Beryl, for pushing me toward the local restaurant at a tender age in search of work. To Chef David R.I.P… it's all your fault, you started it!… but WOW, thanks for a splendid introduction to this, our profession my friend.

Cheers to all the great guys I've worked with… that's the best bit. It's where all the knowledge and tricks of the trade are shared and swapped… there is no substitute for experience.

To the producers and suppliers featured within… thank you – your enthusiasm and welcoming smiles brighten up every meeting. You are creating and supplying quality products of which we should all be proud. Seigi and all at Guernsey Herbs, Kev at Castel Farm Eggs, Andrew Tabel and all at Guernsey Dairy, Fenella, James and his dog Scrumpy, Herbie the Wine Fellow, Dobbo of K Roberts Fisheries, Ray Watts of Meadow Court Farm and of course Jason and Matthew of Porky's… this is for you.

A big thank you also to all my other suppliers, trust me, there are many more but we can't forget to mention Martyn and Colin at Phoenix Fish, Dave the butcher, Shaun 'Sticky' Staples and Gary for their endless support and John Mahy for his daily dairy deliveries. Nigel and Peter of Milton Produce and Roger (Fig Man) Beausire, who also grows the Island's best Guernsey lilies, scented like chocolate.

A huge vote of thanks must also go to The Pavilion team, whom without of course I could not have completed, let alone contemplated, this project. To Tomas Gudelis and Paul Falla, both front of house, for holding the fort in my absence. To Chef René Bisson for all the back-up, whether it was weighing out all the ingredients, preparing the dishes or proof-reading many of the recipes – all in addition to his normal supervision of The Pavilion kitchen. Both Rene and Raimond Gladevics were always there when needed.

This must be the page with the most text. And let's keep it that way from this point forward, because a book like this is nothing without pictures in plenty. So my biggest thank you of all must go to Ally Clark for his wonderful photography. Following a chance meeting I talked him into getting involved and how pleased I am that he did. Ally, it's been a fun learning curve. One where two senses of humour made the whole journey a lot easier.

Finally, and by no means least, a big thank you to all our regular customers and visitors to The Pavilion. You've made it what it is.

FOREWORD
BY BRIAN TURNER CBE

For many years the top chefs of London looked forward with much enthusiasm to their annual trip to Guernsey, the highlight of their year. This was not only for the networking amongst kindred spirits, pals they hadn't seen for a while nor for the socialising with the locals and the opportunity to enjoy good drinking sessions but primarily to be able to assess the great gastronomic progress that was being made in those days.

Our job was to go and dine in the restaurants and hotel dining rooms around the island and to give a view on the quality of food that was being presented to locals and tourists alike. The competition to be awarded the title restaurant 'king' of Guernsey was very fiercely fought, many of the names being in the frame on a regular basis.

It was 1997 when the name Tony Leck was first mentioned, a young upstart with a very different view of competitions. This was in fact the first year of the Guernsey Eating Experience and Tony was chef of the Atlantic Hotel and of 50 entrants the Atlantic came top.

Tony Leck really hit the headlines when he opened The Pavilion, a jewel in Guernsey's crown, hidden away in a beautiful garden and nature reserve. The Pavilion was awarded the overall winner of Guernsey Restaurant of the Year in 2000, in its first year in business what a feat.

Tony has competed in many competitions worldwide but what he really does best is cook in his beloved Pavilion. Desserts are a must in this restaurant where Tony's skill as a pastry chef really shines. Homemade bread, Guernsey Gâche with apples and Guernsey cream and his chocolate tart cannot be missed, but there again the Bean Jar with ham hock and the roast local beef brisket also make my mouth water.

The Pavilion goes from strength to strength, this collection of regional recipes will tell you why, read, cook and enjoy, you know it makes sense!

Brian Turner

Written by: Tony Leck at;

The Pavilion
Guernsey
Tel: 01481 264165
www.thepavilion.co.gg

Edited by:

Martin Edwards – RMC Books
Chris Brierley, Carmel Stewart,
Tel: 0114 2506300

Design by:

Paul Cocker – RMC Books
Alastair Ronaldson
Tel: 0114 2506300

Photography by:

Ally Clark – www.allyclarkphotography.com
Tel: 07781 466503

First Published in 2011 on behalf of:
The Pavilion

Published by:
RMC Books – www.rmcbooks.co.uk

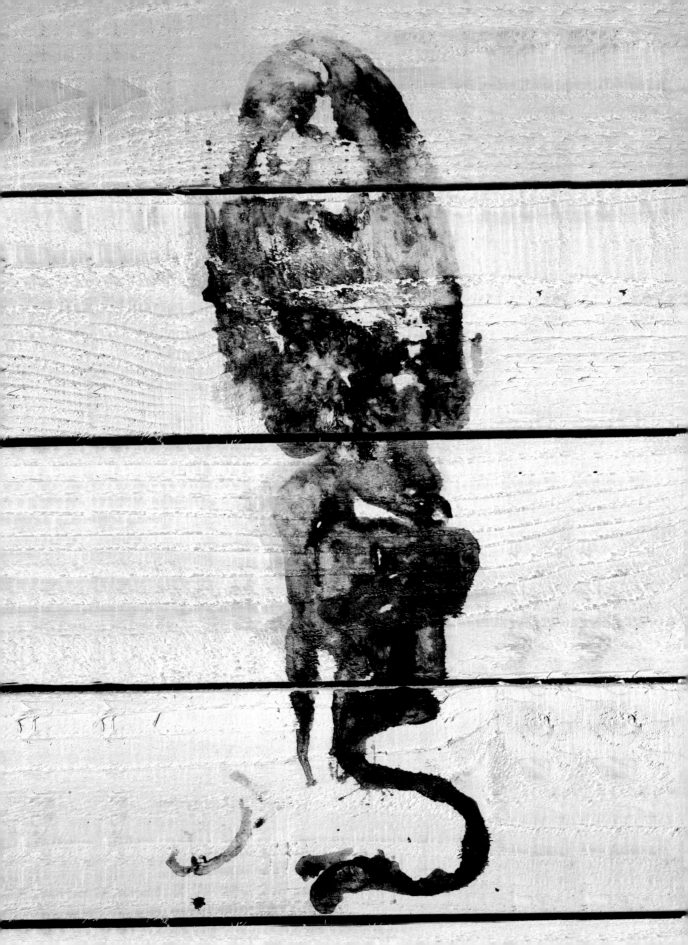

CONTENTS

Acknowledgements 2

Foreword by Brian Turner CBE 5

Credits 6

Contents 9

The Pavilion 10

Hedgeveg 17

Rocquette Cider Company 21

SOUPS AND STARTERS

'Cynful Ale' 'n' Onion Soup 24

Cider & Red Onion Soup 26

Chilled Tomato Consommé 28

Baked 'Frie D'or' in a box 30

Wild Garlic Soup 31

Crab Chowder 32

Spider Crab Bisque 34

Beetroot, Orange & Hazelnut Salad 36

Ham Hock Terrine 38

Oysters with Shallot & Red Wine Dressing 42

Poached Oysters with
Smoked Salmon & Cucumber 43

Asparagus Spears, Poached Free Range
Egg, Ham Croquette 44

Fort Grey Cheese 46

VEGETARIAN DISHES

Apple & Walnut Tart 50

Baked Castel Farm Eggs 51

Potato Peel Pie 52

Fennel Salad 54

Mushroom Duxelle Tart,
Poached Quails' Eggs & Asparagus 55

Beetroot Risotto with Soft Goats Cheese 56

Warm Goats' Cheese Terrine 58

Poached Pear in Mulled Spices
and Blue Cheese Dip 59

K Roberts Fisheries 62

SEAFOOD DISHES

Lobster Salad 64

Crab Salad 66

Lobster Thermidor 68

Fisherman's Scotch Eggs 70

Scallops with Black Pudding Bonbons,
Green Pea Purée 72

Brill Fillet with Wild Mushroom 'Vraic' 74

Skate Wing with Caper Mash,
Parsley & Beetroot, Lemon Butter 76

Mussels with Cider, Cream & Coriander 78

Sea Bass Fillet, Cider
and Seafood Minestrone 80

Mackerel Fillets with Gooseberries 82

Poached Haddock, Baby Spinach
Risotto, Hollandaise Sauce 84

Ormers 86

Traditional Ormer Casserole 88

Crab Cakes 90

Cuttlefish with Ink Risotto and Chorizo 92

Crab Risotto 94

Salt 'n' Pepper Squid with Chilli Dressing 96

C.L.T. Sandwich 98

Fish in Beer Batter 100

Guernsey Fresh Herbs 102

Porky's 108

MEAT DISHES

Pavilion's Traditional Guernsey Bean Jar 112

Braised Lamb Shanks, Red Wine Sauce 114

Mous'Sark'a 116

Boiled Ham with White Onion Sauce 119

Belly Pork, Barbequed Cider Sauce 120

Poached Leg of Mutton with Caper Sauce 122

Loin of Pork with Bayeux Mustard Sauce 123

Meadow Court Farm 124

Brisket of Beef with Chasseur Sauce 128

Fillet Steak, Blue Cheese Bonbons,
Mushroom Duxelle 130

Beef 'n' 'Cynful Ale' Pie 132

Meatballs with Tomato & Basil Sauce 136

Guernsey Dairy 138

DESSERTS

Crème Caramel 140

Lemon Crème Brûlée 142

Lemon & Vanilla Shortbread 143

Rhubarb Pannacotta with Fried Custard 144

Milk a Punch 146

Milk a Punch Pannacotta 146

Chilled Strawberry Rice Pudding 147

Strawberry Shortcake 148

Peppered Strawberries with
Butter Biscuits & Basil Ice Cream 150

Apple & Calvados Baba with
Nutmeg Ice Cream 151

Baked Custard Tart with Nutmeg 152

Lemon Tart 154

Raspberry Arctic Roll
with Summer Berries 156

Floating Islands 158

Cider Cheesecake 160

Traditional Guernsey Gâche Melée
with Marmalade Ice Cream 162

Warm Gâche Melée Cheesecake 164

Guernsey Gâche 'n' Butter Pudding with
Cider Custard 166

Poached Garden Pears with Hedgerow
Brambles 168

Fig & Almond Tart, Honey
& Lavender Cream 170

Dark Chocolate Tart 172

Dark Chocolate & Orange Mousse 174

Dark Chocolate Mousse
with Hedgerow Berries 174

Dark Chocolate Truffle Cake 175

AFTERNOON TEA

Fruity Teacake 176

Victoria Sandwich 178

Fresh Cherry Scones 179

Carrot Cake 180

Traditional Guernsey Gâche 182

Castel Farm Eggs 184

Larder 188-213

Ice Creams 210-213

Ally Clark 217

Recipe index 220

That's shallot! 224

THE PAVILION

Good food has been my passion for as long as I can remember. But it was in Guernsey that I found inspiration.

Unlike many chefs, there was no sudden moment of epiphany. I did not develop a love of cooking in the kitchen alongside my grandmother – although it was from her that I learned the importance of using fresh ingredients. Nor was there a mentor or teacher who set me on the road to where I find myself today.

In my case, there was a steadily-growing appreciation and understanding of how food should be prepared and what it should taste like. I learned more about what goes into cooking as part of my everyday life. My family reared pigs and grew their own tomatoes and salad. In an era when defrosted cheesecake and frozen arctic roll were the desserts of choice, when little silver aliens on television assured us that adding water to reconstitute dried potato was a 'smashing' idea…I thought 'no'.

And so it was that I began my working life as little more than a schoolboy in a restaurant kitchen near home. My first job was washing up, but I watched, listened and learned the ways of the kitchen.

I was born and brought up in the Lake District fishing village of Flookburgh. It was where my grandfather used to work on the sands fishing with the aid of his horse and cart. There were days when the whole family and neighbours banded together to pick shrimps in my grandmother's cottage. Some local people would sell fresh fish, mainly plaice or flounder, known as 'flukes' from the name of the village.

My path in life was set. After leaving school at 16, I was off to study catering at college in Kendal, working evenings and weekends as well. After two years came the big challenge with a move to London.

It was here that I really began to grow as a chef. Encouraged by the head chef, I continued my studies. I think he saw something in me that no-one else – not even I – had noticed. So, following his advice I enrolled on an advanced course at Thames Valley University under the Swiss chef patissier Jean Huber, who taught me the art of creating patisserie.

It was a thoroughly enjoyable course which was far more complex than I expected. I learned about sugar and ice carving and how to work with chocolate. The delicate work appealed to my creative side but at the same time it has a scientific basis so there are set rules which must be followed for it to be a success.

A beautifully-created delicate pudding can be very satisfying because people view it as a treat. The chef's reward is the smile when the dish is presented to them.

For me, cooking is not just about gathering together the best ingredients and putting them together into a simple meal. It is about creating something which is pleasing to look at as well as showcasing the flavours. It's really about job satisfaction. We take the raw ingredients and turn them into something which satisfies all the senses. Cooking must be the only creative profession where as soon as you make something, you want someone to come along and destroy it.

In 1987 I moved to Guernsey, where I worked first as a patisserie chef, and loved the place from the start. There was the thrill of discovering the delights of fresh Guernsey produce to name but one thing. Then there's that easier pace of life – aided by the 35mph speed limit. I continued to learn about food and extend my culinary knowledge by working in various establishments eventually becoming Head Chef. Like many, the next stage seemed to be taking the huge leap and running my own business.

This we did at the turn of the century when we created The Pavilion. It was a good move. In 2000, its first year, our restaurant won the title 'Guernsey Restaurant of the Year', an award presented by Brian Turner CBE. It was particularly pleasing because, unlike all the other establishments in the running, we opened at lunchtimes only.

The Pavilion is set in the beautiful countryside of Guernsey in the Parish of St Saviour, a few miles from St Peter Port, in 8 acres of garden adjacent to a Nature Reserve. We cater for morning coffees and afternoon teas whilst still focusing on lunch. It is a pattern which suits both me and the staff very well. They have time to source the best ingredients, to create new dishes and learn new skills. I work closely with the front-of-house staff, two chefs and an assistant, all of whom have been with me for several years.

The opening hours also allow me to be involved in food events around the island and elsewhere. I am a strong believer in competition and setting challenges for myself and my staff. The result has been a raft of culinary plaudits including a much-coveted Michelin Bib Gourmand which we have retained each and every year since the first 'introduction' or visit in 2004.

The philosophy behind The Pavilion's award-winning menu is KIS – keep it simple. We use fresh, locally-sourced ingredients and I count many of our suppliers among my friends as well as business contacts. The only things which are sent from the mainland are dried goods, spices and oil. Pretty well everything else can be found on the island.

The fruits of that close working relationship can be found on the pages of this book. I hope it gives a flavour of the special place that is Guernsey.

AMOROSA VINE TOMATOES
250 Gm. £1-00

FRESH-LOC...
VEG

PLEASE
PAY HER...

LOBSTER
CRAB & S...
FRESH FISH

MEADOW COURT
FARM

Parish of St. Saviour

Ruette de La Bataille

Leads to

St. Apolline's Chapel
(14th Century)

Pedestrians only

THE BIG FIELD

Area 5.63 acres.
Purchased 2009.
Planted February 2010.

1 yr old maidens on 2 yr root stock.
From trees newly bred seedlings.

AMANDA - Code blue - Root Stock MM106
Good balance, strong growing.

3 COUNTIES - Code Green - Root Stock MM111
Good balance, strong growing.

HELENS - Code Red - Root Stock MM106
High tannic strong growing.

These are 3 early cropping varieties ready for harvesting
last week in September, first week in October

This field has been planted out as an organic orchard from
the outset. One metre wide strips of permeable membrane
has been laid through which the trees have been planted.
This is experimental and as far as we know has never
been done before on a commercial scale.

guernsey
grown

BROAD BEANS £1.50
RUNNER BEANS £1-50
CARROTS £1-20
BEETROOT £1-20

All Veg. sold at this stall is
grown in Guernsey. Without the use of
chemical pesticides. herbicides or fertilizers

Skate Wing
...aper batter new potatoes &
salad or fries

Salt & Pepper Squ...
with summer salad
& thai chilli dressin...
Diver caught loca...
garlic butt...

HEDGEVEG

Drive along the narrow lanes of Guernsey and it won't be long before you see one. They are unique to the island, and form part of the bond that unites its inhabitants.

I'm talking about the 'Hedgeveg' stands, makeshift stalls laden with a glorious array of vegetables, fruits, homemade jams and a variety of produce.

Look out for them by the side of the road, usually accompanied by a hand-written sign detailing the delights on offer and how much payment you are requested to leave... yes, you read that correctly. You'll find a message cordially inviting you to put the correct amount of money in the 'honesty box' next to the goods.

And it's not just a rural custom. Such stalls can even be found in St Peter Port, the island's capital.

Such is the diversity of local growers that all manner of produce is available. Guernsey's tomato-growing industry once dominated local horticulture with more than a thousand acres of glasshouses across the island. It supplied the majority of tomatoes used by British families but the market sadly declined when imports became readily available at cheaper prices from Holland and other countries.

Growers here have now opted to produce other varieties of fruit and vegetables. When a crop is ready and at its prime, any excess is offered for sale from these Hedgeveg stalls.

Throughout the seasons it is not uncommon to find cauliflowers, courgettes, carrots, onions, varieties of beans, peppers, cabbages, squash, artichokes, asparagus, beetroot and not forgetting potatoes. As for tomatoes, not for nothing is Guernsey renowned for what it produces. Expect to find every variety – plum, cherry, cherry plum, red, green and yellow, not to mention a vast array of salad ingredients available too.

Summer fruits to be found at these stalls include succulent strawberries, raspberries, loganberries, tayberries, blackcurrants, redcurrants, gooseberries, kiwi fruits, physalis and even melons. In later months we are blessed with peaches, plums, apricots, figs, blackberries, apples, pears and greengages.

Occasionally it's even possible to find pots covered with hessian sack cloth containing spider or chancre crabs, each marked with the price on their shell. Some stalls offer flowers or a selection of homemade jams, honey, pickles chutneys and marmalades – all perfect for stocking up your larder.

ROCQUETTE CIDER

It was a falling apple that provided a moment of inspiration for Isaac Newton. In a flash, the law of gravity came into being and the rest, as they say, is history.

In the same way, apples feature large in the life of James Meller. And it was pure chance that led him to create what is now one of Guernsey's most distinctive products

The Rocquette Cider Company – a family run business – began in a very small way with a field and that chance meeting with a cider producer from the UK. It just so happened that James bought a property with fields used for grazing cattle. He had been wanting to put them to good use. The cider maker encouraged him and the company was born in 1998.

It began with 2,000 trees and gradually increased that to 3,000. Last year another 1,500 were added to cope with the extra demand. In their first year, they ran out of cider but have never allowed that to happen again. They are now expecting a higher yield as the trees mature.

James said; "We have no rival cider makers in Guernsey but it is quite difficult to produce commercially. Only recently have we reached the stage where we are producing large volumes. Not only has it taken a while to establish a market but also trees take time to grow so it is not the sort of enterprise that anyone can rush into.

"In the early days we had a small amount of labour-intensive equipment. It took a couple of days to press the few kilograms of apples. Now we have industrial presses which can press 100 tonnes of apples in 15 days. But we were producing a quality product from day one because we got the right advice very early on. We began with bottled cider at 6% alcohol but the majority of our business now is 4.5% draught cider which we keg ourselves.

"We have a special recipe and the perfect climate. We produce small sweet cider apples – Dabinett, Michelin and the famous Bramley – which are helped by the Guernsey sunshine, long hours of daylight and mild winters," said James, who is always accompanied by his pet dog Scrumpy.

Even now there is only a small workforce, with three employees to help him – and just one of them is full-time. "It's only when we harvest that I rope in a team to help. In fact, I ask anyone I can find willing to pick apples all day every day from September through to mid-November.

"We also produce a limited special, namely Bec du Nez, a still cider for Sark's annual summer music festival."

I use Rocquette cider in both sweet and savoury dishes. Many recipes benefit from a lighter crisp flavour as an alternative to white wine, whilst the clean flavours cut through some cream-based desserts.

James and I frequently meet at events promoting Guernsey produce. Most of the Rocquette Cider Company's produce is consumed on the island but a small amount is exported to Scotland. If you can't get hold of the real thing any good quality cider will suffice provided it has similar alcohol content and full-bodied flavour.

Soup... a four letter word we all like! One that just conjures up memories for one and all; the great thing about soups is that they can be enjoyed as a starter or as a main meal simply by adjusting the portion size together with chosen accompaniments.

Every café, bistro, restaurant and tearoom – even the odd takeaway - has soup on its menu offering somewhere. It must be up there as one of the original 'fast foods'. All it involves is taking something seasonal that is both at its prime and relatively inexpensive and creating a simple meal from it… the world is your 'oyster soup'!

GUERNSEY 'CYNFUL ALE' 'N' ONION SOUP

Serves 6

METHOD:

Heat a large saucepan and when very hot add the vegetable oil. Immediately add the butter together with the finely sliced onions, chopped garlic and smoked bacon.

Reduce the heat and cook for 15-20 minutes, stirring occasionally until the onions are soft in texture, yet golden brown in colour.

Add to this the cognac and ignite or flambé until all the alcohol has burnt out.

Add the flour and stir well with a wooden spoon; as the mixture begins to thicken add the ale and bring to boiling point. Allow the liquid to reduce by half its volume before adding the meat stock.

Simmer for about 30 minutes, skimming the surface of any scum that may rise to the top.

Season the soup with salt and pepper to taste prior to serving.

Serve with garlic and mature cheddar croutes.

To prepare the croutes, cut slices of bread and place upon baking sheet. Sprinkle each with a little olive oil and grill, turn each one over and repeat. Rub each croute with a little garlic and then sprinkle with grated cheddar before grilling again to melt the cheese.

INGREDIENTS:

30g	Unsalted Guernsey butter
2 tbsp	Vegetable oil
1kg	Onions (peeled & finely shredded)
30g	Smoked bacon (chopped)
30g	Flour
1	Clove garlic (chopped)
750ml	'Cynful Ale' (or your preferred local ale)
750ml	Beef stock (see page 188)
25ml	Cognac
100g	Mature Guernsey cheddar
	Sliced bread for croutes
	Sea salt
	Freshly ground pepper

ROCQUETTE CIDER AND RED ONION SOUP WITH GUERNSEY BRIE CROUTONS

Serves 6 – A local variation on French onion soup

INGREDIENTS:

750g	Sliced red onions
2	Large cooking apples (peeled, cored & diced)
100ml	Rocquette cider
500ml	Good clear beef stock (see page 188)
50g	Guernsey butter
	Sea salt
	Freshly ground black pepper
	Caster sugar
150g	Guernsey brie
1	Egg
	Plain flour
	Dried ground breadcrumbs or ground almonds

METHOD:

Peel and slice the red onions very thinly. Season well with salt, freshly ground black pepper and a sprinkle of caster sugar. Combine with the diced apples and set aside for an hour.

Cut the brie into wedges. Coat in flour, dip into the beaten egg and finally the breadcrumbs or almonds to ensure an even coating.

Place the onion and apple mixture into a thick-bottomed pan with the butter and cook slowly and gently until the onion is very soft.

Add the beef stock together with the Rocquette cider and bring to the boil. Simmer gently for several minutes before adjusting the seasoning to taste.

Deep fry the brie wedges in hot vegetable oil until golden. Drain on kitchen paper to absorb any excess fat before serving.

CHILLED GUERNSEY TOMATO CONSOMMÉ, SUMMER VEGETABLES AND FRESH GUERNSEY HERBS

Serves 6

INGREDIENTS:

Consommé

1000g	Overripe tomatoes
50g	Basil (chopped)
70g	Chervil (chopped)
40g	Tarragon (chopped)
100ml	Dry white wine
1	Shallot (finely chopped)
1 bunch	Flat leaf parsley
	Sea salt
	Freshly ground pepper
5g	Caster sugar

Summer Vegetables

50g	Tomato
50g	Shelled peas
50g	Carrot
50g	Courgette
50g	Broad beans (peeled)

Garnish:

Shredded tarragon, chervil and basil leaves

METHOD:

Use overripe tomatoes, preferably purchased still on the vine. Roughly chop and place in a large bowl or saucepan with the chopped herbs, shallot and white wine.

Squeeze the tomatoes until crushed and season lightly. Place all the ingredients into a large muslin cloth and tie together. Hang over a large container in the refrigerator overnight.

Once the juices have drained from the muslin cloth, strain once more through a fine sieve and keep chilled.

Prepare the summer vegetables by blanching each variety separately and cutting into desired shape. Add these to the consommé and adjust seasoning to taste.

Season with caster sugar if desired.

Serve chilled, garnished with freshly shredded herbs.

BAKED 'FRIE D'OR' IN A BOX

Serves 2 as a starter to share

INGREDIENTS:

200g	Guernsey Dairy Frie d'Or cheese (or Camembert)
25ml	Port
20g	Fresh Guernsey thyme
	Sea salt
	Freshly ground black pepper
	Olive oil
	Freshly baked bread
	Freshly picked Guernsey baby leaf salad

METHOD:

Pre-heat the oven to 200°C, 400°F, Gas 6.

Unwrap the Frie d'Or and with a sharp knife remove the rind from the top of the cheese. Put the cheese back in the box and season with sea salt, black pepper and freshly-picked thyme. Sprinkle generously with a quality olive oil and a splash of port. Place in the oven for 10-15 minutes.

Serve with some crusty freshly baked bread and baby leaf salad.

Camembert in a box can be used as an alternative.

WILD GARLIC SOUP

Serves 4

INGREDIENTS:

25g	Guernsey Dairy butter
100ml	Guernsey Dairy whipping cream
1	Onion (finely diced)
½	Garlic clove (crushed)
25g	Fresh Guernsey parsley
450g	New season potatoes
500ml	Chicken or vegetable stock (see page 189/190)
500g	Wild garlic leaves (washed)
	Sea salt
	Freshly ground white pepper

METHOD:

Melt the butter in a heavy-based saucepan over a moderate heat, fry the chopped garlic and onion, stirring regularly until the onion is soft but not coloured. Add the washed and scrubbed new season potatoes and seasoning. Pour in the vegetable or chicken stock and cook until the potatoes are almost cooked through. Remove approximately half of the potatoes and cool in chilled water. When cool, dice the potatoes ready to add prior to serving.

Add the wild garlic and chopped parsley to the liquid and cook for a further 2 minutes. Blitz the soup using a blender and pass through a sieve. Finally stir in the cream and add diced potatoes. Serve immediately.

Wild garlic is an early spring foraging favourite, found along hedgerows and in shaded areas. There are various guises; (allium ursinum), often known as 'stinking onions' or ramsons, it is a wild relative of chives. If you are unsure whether you have foraged the correct plant, its wonderful aroma will confirm you're on the right track.

Wild garlic can give extra flavour to an abundance of dishes and salads or can be prepared into a wild garlic pesto.

GUERNSEY CRAB CHOWDER

Serves 6

INGREDIENTS:

284ml	Guernsey Dairy whipping cream
250ml	Guernsey Dairy milk
500ml	Fish stock
250ml	Rocquette cider
450g	White crab meat
200g	Brown crab meat
250g	Onions (finely diced)
1	Garlic clove (diced)
25g	Guernsey butter
30g	Plain flour
450g	New season potatoes
100g	Smoked bacon
20g	Fresh Guernsey thyme
20g	Fresh Guernsey chives
	Sea Salt
	Freshly ground white pepper

METHOD:

Peel or scrape clean the potatoes. Dice into 1cm sized pieces and set aside.

Pick through the white crab meat to ensure any traces of shell are removed.

Using a pastry scraper, force the brown crab meat through a fine sieve. Set both the brown and white crab meat aside in the refrigerator until required.

Dice the smoked bacon and place in a heavy-based saucepan together with the onion, garlic and the butter. Gently cook for 4-5 minutes over a moderate heat without colouring until the onions soften and become translucent. Add the flour and cook for a further 2-3 minutes to form a roux.

In a separate saucepan, heat the fish stock together with the cider and milk.

Gradually add this hot liquid to the roux, stirring continuously to prevent any lumps forming. Add the potatoes to the liquid together with the cream and sprigs of freshly picked thyme. Cook gently until the potatoes are just tender. Add both the picked white crab meat together with the sieved brown meat and stir. Season to taste and serve hot, sprinkled with some freshly chopped chives.

SPIDER CRAB BISQUE

Serves 6

INGREDIENTS:

1.5kg	Fresh live crab (alternatively replace with live lobsters)
50g	Guernsey butter
1	Large carrot
3	Sticks celery
1	Large onion
1	Fennel bulb
1	Medium leek
1	Clove of garlic
6	Ripe tomatoes
120g	Tomato purée
250ml	White wine
125ml	Dry vermouth
1500ml	Fish stock (see page 191)
50ml	Cognac
125ml	Guernsey whipping cream
	Tarragon
	Thyme
	Olive oil
1	Lemon
	Sea salt
	Freshly ground white pepper

METHOD:

To despatch the spider crab either place in a freezer for a couple of hours or simply pierce the air sac with a sharp knife. Alternatively, plunge into a large pan of boiling salted water for about 10 minutes – some say seawater is best.

Take off the top of the shell, remove the grit sac and gills and discard them. Cut the crab into smaller pieces with a large knife. Heat olive oil in a large heavy-based pan until almost smoking and cook the vegetables, crab and garlic for 10-15 minutes until lightly caramelised. Add the cognac and flambé until all the alcohol has burnt off. Add the tomatoes and tomato purée and cook whilst stirring for a further 10 minutes. Add the white wine and vermouth. Return to boiling point and simmer until volume has reduced by half.

Cover with the pre-prepared fish stock and sprigs of herbs. Simmer gently for up to 2 hours. Skim the surface of any scum which may form during this period.

Liquidise the soup in batches or use a large hand blender to blitz before passing through a sieve at least twice. Pour into a clean saucepan and continue to simmer until the bisque slightly thickens. Add the cream and season with sea salt and freshly ground white pepper. A squeeze of lemon juice will help bring the flavours out.

Serve with freshly baked homemade crusty bread or Guernsey biscuits. (See page 201)

BEETROOT, ORANGE & HAZELNUT SALAD WITH ROCKET AND PARMESAN

Serves 4 as a starter

INGREDIENTS:

1kg	Raw beetroot
250g	Fresh Guernsey rocket salad
2	Large oranges
75g	Parmesan cheese
50g	Roasted hazelnuts
50g	Beetroot leaves
	Olive oil
	Balsamic glaze
	Freshly ground black pepper
	Unbleached coarse sea salt

METHOD:

Thoroughly wash the whole fresh beetroot, reserving any of the leaves for use within the salad. Place the beets in a large saucepan and cover with salted water. Bring to boiling point and discard the water. Replenish with fresh water and bring to boiling point once again. Simmer gently until beets are just cooked yet still firm. Allow to cool in the cooking liquor. Reserve the liquor for use in other dishes such as the beetroot risotto. (See page 56)

To roast the hazelnuts, spread out on a baking tray in a hot oven or under the grill until the skins blister. Alternatively, place in a dry saucepan and gently heat. Remove the hazelnuts and place on a clean tea towel. Roll the cloth around between your hands – this will loosen the hazelnut skins.

Wash the oranges before removing the zest using a fine grater or zester. Remove the orange segments with a sharp knife.

Prepare a dressing for the salad with olive oil, balsamic glaze, any excess orange juice and zest of orange. Season to taste.

Assemble the salad by roughly cutting the beetroot into the desired shapes. Toss the beetroot in a large bowl together with the rocket and skinned hazelnuts. Drizzle on the prepared dressing and finally shave some parmesan cheese over the top with a vegetable peeler.

HAM HOCK TERRINE WITH PARSLEY & CAPER PRESSING

Serves 6-8 as a starter

INGREDIENTS:

2	Ham hocks (approximately 2kg)
1	Large carrot (chopped)
1	Stick of celery (chopped)
1	Large onion (chopped)
1	Medium leek
1	Cooking apple
1	Whole clove
1	Bunch parsley stalks

Parsley & Caper Pressing:

100g	Fresh Guernsey flat leaf parsley (chopped)
50g	Fine capers (drained)
	Freshly ground white pepper
	Bayeux mustard (optional)

METHOD:

To remove some of the saltiness of the ham hocks, soak the joints overnight in cold water, changing the water once or twice.

The following day place the hocks in a large saucepan; add the chopped celery, carrot, leeks, whole apple and the onion. Cover with fresh water and bring to the boil. Skim any scum from the surface and continue to cook on a simmering boil for up to 3 hours or until cooked.

Ensure the joints are covered at all times with water when cooking. Allow the hocks to cool naturally in the cooking liquor. Remove from the liquor and pick the meat from the bones, discarding any excess fat and skin. The skin can be dried on a

baking tray in a low oven and pressed or rolled out to create pork scratching for use in other dishes. The amount of ham hock retained may have reduced in weight by up to 55per cent once the bones etc. have been discarded. The ham stock can also be retained for preparation in other recipes.

Mix together the picked hock meat with chopped flat leaf parsley and chopped capers, season with freshly ground white pepper.

Layer a terrine mould with cling wrap. Place the hock mixture into the terrine and wrap the whole terrine with more cling wrap, place a heavy weight upon the terrine and refrigerate until set. Slice the terrine when required and serve with a seasonal fresh Guernsey herb salad and Bayeux mustard dressing prepared by mixing Bayeux grain mustard with mayonnaise or with our piccalilli recipe. (See page 195)

OYSTERS

Once you have purchased your oysters, store them in a refrigerator, preferably on crushed ice and covered with a damp clean cloth. If possible store them upright, with the round bases of the shell at the bottom. This will allow all the natural juices to be retained in the base of the shell when opened.

Lay each oyster (one at a time) on a folded cloth or tea towel on a flat surface. With the flat part of the shell facing upwards, hold very firmly with one hand, using part of the cloth to protect your hand in case you slip!

As with all jobs, this task will be made a great deal easier – not to mention safer – by using the correct tools. An oyster knife with a guard attached is perfect.

Force the point of an oyster knife into the hinge part of the oyster, carefully moving the knife from side to side until the shell is prised open.

Once the shell feels as if it is about to be released, run the knife around the top of the flat shell and twist slightly. This will act on the muscle that connects the oyster to the shell. Lift off the top half of the shell and discard.

Being very careful not to lose any of the oyster juices, remove any fragments of shell from the flesh. The oyster meat will still be connected to the rounded base; this is simply cut by running the oyster knife under the flesh.

FRESH HERM OYSTERS
WITH SHALLOT & RED WINE DRESSING

Serves 4 as a starter

INGREDIENTS:

24	Herm oysters
250ml	Cabernet Sauvignon
2	Shallots (finely diced)
175ml	Ruby port
75ml	Red wine vinegar
5g	Fresh Guernsey tarragon (chopped)
5g	Fresh Guernsey dill (chopped)
	Juice of half a lemon
	Freshly cracked black peppercorns
	Hot pepper sauce (optional)

METHOD:

Open the oysters and reserve both the meat and any liquid, rinse the rounded bases of the shell and place on crushed ice or an oyster dish.

In a saucepan, bring the red wine, ruby port and half of the red wine vinegar to the boil and simmer until the liquid has reduced in volume to almost a syrup. Remove from the heat and allow to cool.

Finely chop the shallots, tarragon and dill, add the remaining red wine vinegar to this. Once the syrup is cold, add to the other ingredients and serve alongside the oysters in a bowl.

Serve with freshly cracked peppercorns, fresh lemon and an optional splash of hot pepper sauce.

POACHED HERM OYSTERS
WITH SMOKED SALMON & CUCUMBER

Serves 4 as a starter

INGREDIENTS:

24	Herm oysters
100g	Guernsey Dairy unsalted butter
60ml	Guernsey Dairy whipping cream
125ml	Dry white wine
150g	Smoked salmon (finely sliced into matchsticks)
1	Cucumber (finely sliced into matchsticks)
20g	Fresh Guernsey chives
	Juice of half a lemon
	Freshly ground black pepper

METHOD:

Pre-heat the oven to 275°F, 140°C or Gas 1.

Cut the butter into small dice and return to a cold refrigerator.

Open the oysters and remove the meat, setting aside in the refrigerator until required. Reserve all the oyster liquid and place in a saucepan with the dry white wine.

Wash the rounded base of the shells and place in a serving dish. Put the serving dish in the bottom of the oven to warm.

Bring the wine and liquor to boiling point. Reduce the heat, add the oyster meat and simmer for about 1 minute. Remove the meat and set aside. Turn up the heat and boil until the liquid has reduced to 2-3 teaspoons in volume. Add the Guernsey cream and reduce until the sauce begins to thicken slightly.

In a separate saucepan, melt 10-15g of butter and lightly toss the strips of smoked salmon and cucumber, season with freshly-ground black pepper and set to one side, keeping warm.

Meanwhile, remove the thickened sauce from the heat and whisk in the pre-diced cold butter a little at a time to emulsify the sauce. Don't be tempted to hurry the process. If too much is added too quickly or if the butter melts too fast then the sauce could separate.

Once the sauce has emulsified, add the oyster meat. Check seasoning and spoon into pre-warmed shells. Sprinkle with a little of the sautéed smoked salmon and cucumber. Add a generous sprinkling of finely chopped fresh chives before serving.

ASPARAGUS SPEARS, POACHED FREE RANGE EGG, HAM CROQUETTE

Serves 6 as a starter

INGREDIENTS:

1kg	Asparagus
6	Free range eggs
30g	Guernsey butter
	Hollandaise sauce (see page 195)
1 dsp	Malt vinegar

Ham Croquettes:

180g	Mashed potato
140g	Boiled ham (see page 119)
	Egg & milk, flour and breadcrumbs to coat

METHOD:

Prepare the ham croquettes by mixing together the cold pre-prepared mashed potato with diced ham, shape as desired and coat firstly with seasoned flour, followed by dipping in a mixture of beaten egg and milk, finally dip in finely grated breadcrumbs, reshape using a palette knife and reserve in refrigerator until required.

Peel the asparagus from just below the tips to the ends of the stalks with a sharp vegetable peeler.

Bring to the boil some salted water and blanch the asparagus spears for 3-4 minutes or until tender. Remove from water and refresh immediately in chilled water. Set aside the asparagus on some kitchen paper until required.

In another saucepan boil some slightly salted water and add the dessertspoon of malt vinegar. Stir the water in a circular motion to create a mini whirlpool. Crack the free range eggs into the water individually; the moving water will help to retain the shape of the eggs. Poach gently for about 3 minutes.

Melt the butter in a large non-stick frying pan and add the asparagus spears to reheat for about 2 minutes, season well and serve upon warmed plates.

To serve:

Deep-fry the ham croquettes and place on the asparagus. Using a slotted spoon, remove the poached eggs from the water and drain on some kitchen paper. Put each egg on to the asparagus and spoon hollandaise over each plate. Serve immediately.

Asparagus is in season for a very limited period from late April through to early June. Although available year round in supermarkets, fresh is best to ensure the slight sweetness with a nutty flavour.

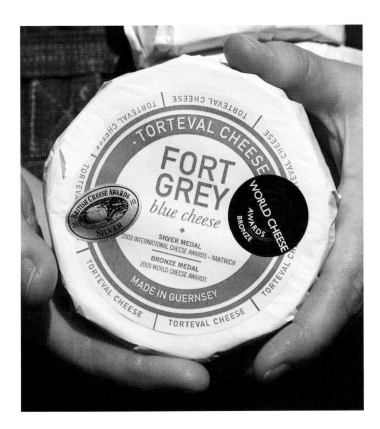

FORT GREY CHEESE

When I ask visitors about their first impressions of Guernsey, there is one word that is guaranteed to feature in the answer. Tranquil, beautiful, idyllic, maybe. But small, certainly.

It's a small island, right enough – 27 miles around with rugged cliffs to the east and north and sandy beaches to the west and south.

The word applies also to everything on it, from the narrow roads to the island's capital, St Peter Port, to the ten parishes that would be called middling hamlets anywhere else. That's a major part of its charm, a reason why it captivates so many people.

In the same way, the inevitably smaller scale of commercial production means there are some things you can only find here. They're just not made in quantities big enough to feature on the mainland market.

A perfect example is Fort Grey cheese. Its driving force, Fenella Maddison, is a producer whose motto could well be small is beautiful. She has resisted any temptation to expand, preferring instead to keep her cheese-making business diminutive and perfectly formed.

She hails from East Sussex where she worked as a nurse, establishing her Torteval Cheese company in her Guernsey garage in 2007 as an old-fashioned cottage industry and there she has remained.

The cheese she makes has changed over time but her methodical, intuitive method remains the same. Her soft blue award-winning vegetarian cheese, made from full fat Guernsey cow's milk, is unlike any other. Think of Blue Brie made in a similar style to Camembert and you are almost there – but not quite. The only real way to experience it is to taste it.

"When I moved here from Lewes I began by producing goats' cheese but gradually found the supply of milk too small for commercial purposes so had to concentrate on cows' milk which was not a problem as it is probably the best milk in the world!" said Fenella.

"All through my nursing career I had wanted to be a self-sufficient smallholder and was increasingly interested in food production. Our move to Guernsey presented me with the perfect opportunity. I went on a couple of courses, gradually acquired the right equipment and, after cluttering up the kitchen for a few months, eventually converted the garage into a cheese room.

"As a child my family had a brief foray into goat ownership so I have a certain fondness for them but they were so naughty they caused marital strife and had to go. We also had pet donkeys which were far less troublesome.

"I have no interest in celebrity culture but I do admire other cheese makers. It is such a small world that you can very easily find yourself talking to one of your heroes. When I first set up, I had no idea what I was doing and had a few disasters but I found other makers were very generous with their advice, which made all the difference. Randolph Hodgson who runs Neal's Yard Dairy was particularly helpful.

"The Fort Grey comes from a very simple recipe which lends itself very well to the rich Guernsey milk – it has proved the perfect combination. Over time I have varied both the ingredients and the preparation but its essence has remained the same."

These unique products bear distinctive Guernsey names. Fort Grey takes its name from the coastal fortification in the far western parish of Torteval, where Fenella and her family live.

APPLE & WALNUT TART
WITH TORTEVAL BLUE CHEESE SAUCE,
BABY GUERNSEY SPINACH & WALNUT SALAD

Serves 6 x 10cm diameter tartlets

INGREDIENTS:

6	Apples (peeled, cored and halved)
250g	Savoury shortcrust pastry (Basic recipe page 206, except don't add the sugar, vanilla or lemon)
30g	Guernsey Dairy unsalted butter
120g	Walnuts
3 or 4	Free range eggs
60g	Self-raising flour
60g	Ground almonds
1	Onion (finely diced)
60g	Torteval 'Fort Grey' blue cheese
	Baby spinach leaves
50ml	Mayonnaise
	Walnut oil

Mulled spice sugar syrup

375ml	Red wine
75g	Caster sugar
1	Cinnamon stick
1	Orange (peel only)
3-4	Cloves

METHOD:

Make a mulled spice sugar syrup by boiling together the red wine, caster sugar, cinnamon, orange peel and cloves then reducing for 5 minutes.

Poach the peeled, cored and halved apples in the syrup and set aside.

Line tart tins with shortcrust pastry and allow to rest for 30 minutes before trimming the edges of any surplus pastry.

Prepare walnut sponge filling by gently cooking one finely-chopped onion in a knob of butter until translucent. Season and add a splash of wine and reduce until it is almost a syrup. Allow to cool.

Place 30g of Guernsey Dairy unsalted butter into food processor with 120g walnuts and blitz.

Slowly add 2-3 eggs. Fold into this mixture self-raising flour, ground almonds and the cooked onion.

Divide equally between tart tins. Place two halves of the poached apple onto each one.

Bake before serving at 160°C, 325°F or Gas 3 for 30-40 minutes.

Serve with Torteval 'Fort Grey' blue cheese sauce (see page 193) and a salad of baby spinach tossed in mayonnaise with a little walnut oil added.

BAKED CASTEL FARM EGGS WITH BABY SPINACH & TORTEVAL BLUE CHEESE SAUCE

Serves 6

INGREDIENTS:

12	Free range eggs
3	Free range egg yolks
1	Onion (finely diced)
75g	Guernsey Dairy butter
750ml	Vegetable stock (see page 190)
50ml	Guernsey Dairy whipping cream
120g	Torteval 'Fort Grey' blue cheese
175g	Baby spinach leaves
	Guernsey fresh herbs

METHOD:

Wash and carefully pat dry the baby spinach leaves. Heat a large saucepan and gently sauté in a little Guernsey Dairy butter. Season with salt, pepper and freshly grated nutmeg. Place the spinach leaves in a colander and allow to drain.

To prepare the Torteval 'Fort Grey' blue cheese sauce, sauté the onion gently in 50g of butter until soft and translucent. Remove from the heat and drain the chopped onion of any excess liquid. In a separate saucepan heat the vegetable stock and reduce in volume by two-thirds, add the sautéed chopped onion, blue cheese and stir until the sauce thickens. Add the Guernsey Dairy whipping cream and reduce to required consistency. Whisk the egg yolks into the sauce and remove from the heat.

Divide and place the drained spinach leaves into the bottom of six ovenproof baking dishes. Crack two eggs into each dish before putting the dishes into a bain-marie and placing in the oven.

Bake when required at 160°C, 325°F or Gas 3 for approximately 30-40 minutes.

When the eggs are set, remove from the oven and bain-marie, pour the blue cheese sauce onto each dish. Place under a hot salamander or grill for 2-3 minutes before serving.

POTATO PEEL PIE

Serves 4

To some this may sound an unappetising dish, yet it's famous in Guernsey following the publication of the novel The Guernsey Literary and Potato Peel Pie Society. The book reflects life during the wartime occupation of the island when food was in very short supply. This is a modern take on the dish using readily available ingredients.

INGREDIENTS:

900g	Potatoes
75g	Guernsey Dairy butter
430ml	Guernsey Dairy whipping cream
1	Onion (finely sliced)
1 clove	Garlic (finely chopped)
1	Spring cabbage
25g	Fresh Guernsey parsley
750ml	Vegetable stock (see page 190)
500g	Wild garlic leaves (washed)
120g	Guernsey Dairy smoked cheese
	Sea salt
	Freshly ground black pepper

METHOD:

Melt half the butter in a heavy-based saucepan over a moderate heat. Add the finely-chopped garlic and sliced onion and stir regularly until the onion becomes soft and translucent.

Add one third of the washed wild garlic and continue to cook gently for 2-3 minutes without colouring. Place all the ingredients in a colander to drain, reserving the excess butter.

Wash the potatoes well and remove the skins with a cheese grater. Soak the grated skins in a little cold water until required. Slice the remainder of the peeled potatoes thinly using a mandolin or sharp cook's knife.

Prepare the cabbage by washing each leaf and removing the core stalks.

Using a large saucepan, bring the vegetable stock to a rapid boil. Drop the cabbage leaves into the stock for a minute to blanch, then remove from the liquid and refresh in cold water. Do the same with the thinly-sliced potatoes.

Pat dry both the blanched potatoes and cabbage using kitchen paper or a cloth before layering a pre-greased oven tray or casserole pot with a thin layer of potatoes, Season well before adding a layer of cabbage followed by a sprinkle of sliced onion. Season each layer with salt and pepper and keep layering until the pot is almost full. Reserve a few slices of potato for the accompanying sauce.

In a separate saucepan, scald two-thirds of the cream and pour over the potatoes. Sprinkle the top with the grated smoked cheddar and place the dish into a hot oven 180°C, 350°F or Gas 4 for 40-50 minutes or until the potato is cooked and the pie is golden.

Remove from the oven and allow to stand for 5-10 minutes before serving.

To serve, gently cook the remaining chopped wild garlic in the butter over a medium heat until soft. Add the reserved potato, the remaining one-third of the cream and boil for 2 minutes. Blitz the sauce and pour through a fine sieve.

The sauce should be a vibrant creamy colour with a mild garlic/onion flavour.

Pat-dry the grated potato skins and deep fry until crisp and golden.

Serve the hot casserole dish of potato pie with the freshly-made wild garlic sauce and sprinkle the crispy potato skins on top to garnish.

FENNEL SALAD

INGREDIENTS:

450g	Fennel bulb
½	Onion (finely sliced)
1	Lemon (zest & juice)
10ml	Cider vinegar
25g	Fresh Guernsey tarragon
25g	Caster sugar
60ml	Olive oil
	Sea salt
	Freshly ground black pepper

METHOD:

Prepare vinaigrette by whisking together the olive oil, cider vinegar, picked tarragon stalks and caster sugar. Adjust acidity with lemon juice and season well with salt and pepper. Set aside until required.

For the fennel bulbs, remove the bottom core and peel the outer layer with a vegetable peeler. Remove each layer or stalk of fennel and slice very thinly using a mandolin.

Peel and slice onion thinly, place both the vegetables in a large stainless steel bowl and toss together with the finely grated lemon zest and the prepared vinaigrette.

Serve as a standalone salad or to accompany other dishes, such as lobster salad (see page 64).

Tony Leck's Pavilion on a Plate

LA VALLEE'S FARM MUSHROOM DUXELLE TART WITH POACHED QUAILS' EGGS, ASPARAGUS & HOLLANDAISE SAUCE

Serves 6 x 10cm diameter tartlets

INGREDIENTS:

Shortcrust savoury pastry:

150g	Plain flour (sieved)
75g	Guernsey Dairy butter
40ml	Iced cold water

Mushroom duxelle:

25g	Guernsey Dairy butter
450g	La Vallee's Farm mushrooms
60g	Shallots (finely chopped)
20g	Fresh Guernsey tarragon
25ml	Madeira wine
50ml	Guernsey Dairy whipping cream

Asparagus & poached egg filling:

500g	Asparagus
18	Quails' eggs
30g	Guernsey butter
	Hollandaise sauce (see page 195)
1 dsp	Malt vinegar

METHOD:

Prepare the pastry by rubbing together the flour and butter until a sandy texture. Add to this the iced water and mix together gently. Divide into six balls and roll each out into approximately 12cm diameter discs. Line each tartlet mould carefully and set aside in the refrigerator to rest for 30 minutes. Prick the base of each tartlet with a fork and line with baking parchment. Fill each tartlet with dried baking beans or rice and trim off any excess overhanging pastry. Bake blind at 165°C, 325°F or Gas 3 until pastry is cooked evenly and golden in colour. Remove from the oven and set aside until required.

For the Mushroom duxelle:

Wash the mushrooms under cold water, pat dry, place in a food processor and blitz.

In a frying pan, gently sauté the chopped shallots in the butter until they soften and become translucent. Add the blitzed mushrooms and cook gently until the liquid has almost evaporated and the mixture begins to thicken. Add the freshly picked tarragon leaves, Madeira wine and Guernsey Dairy cream. Gently reduce the mixture until a paste is almost formed, adjust seasoning and set aside to keep hot.

For the Asparagus & poached egg filling:

Peel the asparagus from just below the tips to the ends of the stalks with a sharp vegetable peeler.

Bring salted water to boiling point and add the asparagus spears for 3-4 minutes, until tender. Remove from water and refresh immediately in chilled water. Set aside on kitchen paper until required.

In another saucepan, boil slightly salted water and add the dessertspoon of malt vinegar. Stir the water in a circular fashion to create a mini whirlpool. Crack the quail's eggs into the water individually. The moving water will help to retain the shape of the eggs. Poach gently for about 45 seconds. Remove the eggs with a slotted spoon and immerse in iced water, retaining the hot poaching water.

Melt the butter in a large non-stick frying pan and add the asparagus spears to reheat for approximately 2 minutes, season well.

To serve, divide the Mushroom Duxelle between the tartlets, add the quail's eggs to the hot water briefly to reheat. Using warmed but not too hot plates, place three quail's eggs on each tartlet together with the asparagus tips. Spoon over the Hollandaise sauce and place under a salamander or hot grill for a couple of minutes until the Hollandaise sauce is glazed. Serve immediately.

BEETROOT RISOTTO
WITH SOFT GOATS' CHEESE

Serves 4

INGREDIENTS:

450g	Cooked beetroot (approx. 4 medium sized)
125g	Chopped onion
280g	Arborio risotto rice
800ml	Beetroot stock (see page 36)
250ml	Dry white wine
25g	Fresh Guernsey thyme
200g	Soft goats' cheese
25ml	Olive oil
	Freshly ground black pepper
	Unbleached coarse sea salt

Salad:

40g	Fresh Guernsey rocket salad
40g	Fresh Guernsey basil leaves
50g	Beetroot leaves
2	Large oranges
50g	Parmesan cheese
50g	Roasted hazelnuts
	Olive oil
	Balsamic glaze

METHOD:

Finely chop the onion and place in a heavy-based saucepan with the thyme and the olive oil. Cook over a medium heat, stirring constantly. Add the rice. Keep stirring until the onion becomes soft and translucent. Pour in the dry white wine a little at a time, stirring with a spatula. Once all the wine is incorporated, start to add the beetroot stock a little at a time, allowing the rice to absorb the liquid whilst still stirring. This will take approximately 20 minutes until the rice is 'al dente' or just cooked.

Cut the beetroot roughly sized pieces and stir in. Cut the soft goats' cheese into equal sized pieces and place in the risotto. Remove from the heat and let the risotto stand for 3-4 minutes. Stir to incorporate all the ingredients and serve into bowls.

Toss the salad leaves together with a little olive oil and balsamic glaze. Combine with the salad, orange segments and toasted hazelnuts. Season to taste and serve with freshly-shaved parmesan cheese.

WARM GOATS' CHEESE TERRINE

Serves 10-12

INGREDIENTS:

400g	Leeks
450g	Goats' Cheese
1500g	Maris Piper potatoes
175g	Guernsey Dairy whipping cream
25g	Guernsey Dairy butter
	Sea salt, freshly grated nutmeg and freshly ground black pepper
	Red onion jam (see page 197)

METHOD:

Trim the goats' cheese log of any crust, place into a bowl and beat well whilst seasoning with freshly ground black pepper and sea salt.

Layer several sheets of cling wrap upon a clean work surface and place this goats' cheese upon it. Reform into a sausage shape approx. the same length as your chosen terrine mould with the help of several layers of cling wrap. Wrap tightly and chill well or place into a freezer for 30 minutes.

Split the leeks lengthways and remove the larger strips. Wash thoroughly before plunging into rapidly boiling seasoned water. Cook in this water for only a matter of seconds before removing and plunging into iced water to refresh the leaves.

Once cold set aside to drain.

Peel the potatoes and cut into roughly sized pieces. Bring to boil in salted water and cook until tender.

Drain off any excess water and return to heat. Add seasoning of sea salt, pepper and freshly grated nutmeg. To this, add some of the whipping cream; the amount required will depend upon how dry the cooked potato is. Proceed to mash the seasoned potato mixture in a rustic fashion or simply leave it half mashed, half whole! To assemble line a terrine or loaf tin with several layers of cling wrap. Line this with the strips of blanched leek leaving lengths of the leek overhanging and season lightly.

Half fill the mould with the potato mixture. Remove the goats' cheese from the chiller, unwrap and place into the centre of your mould, top with remaining potato and overlap with the leek. Wrap the whole dish tightly with more layers of cling wrap. Place into a deep roasting tray and pour into this hot water to half the loaf tins depth. Cover with baking foil and place into a moderate oven for approx. 1 hour. Remove from roasting tray and allow to cool prior to chilling.

To serve, remove from wrapping and slice into required portions, lightly dust one side of each slice with a little flour and place into a hot non-stick frying pan with a knob of Guernsey Dairy butter before placing into a hot oven for 3-4 minutes. Serve with red onion jam and mixed fresh Guernsey herbs & salad leaves.

POACHED GARDEN PEAR IN MULLED SPICES WITH TORTEVAL BLUE CHEESE DIP

Serves 4

 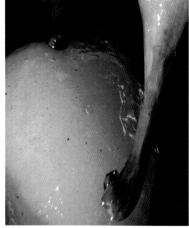 

INGREDIENTS:

4	Pears
75g	Sugar
1	Cinnamon stick
1	Bay leaf
375ml	Red wine
1	Orange (cut into quarters)
3-4	Cloves
100g	Torteval blue cheese
50ml	Guernsey cream
50ml	Vegetable stock (see page 190)
½	Onion (chopped)

METHOD:

Peel and core the pears before placing in a pan of poaching stock prepared from the red wine and sugar, along with the orange and mulled spices.

Poach the pears gently until tender and cool in the liquor, allowing the mulled spices to infuse.

When cool, cut each pear into cubes and place upon kebab skewers ready to serve.

For the Torteval blue cheese dip, gently sauté the chopped onion in a non-stick pan. Add the vegetable stock and reduce in volume by half.

Add the cream and repeat reduction prior to adding grated blue cheese. Cook briefly until the sauce thickens the dip slightly and serve.

The pear kebabs can be served either as they are or reheated, either within the poaching liquor or by roasting briefly in the oven.

Serve with fresh Guernsey herb salad and slices of toasted walnut bread. (See page 205)

Tony Leck's Pavilion on a Plate

K ROBERTS FISHERIES

We men are not famous for our multi-tasking. But Keith Roberts shows that it can be done. Known to all as 'Dobbo', he is out and about early in the morning delivering the daily post in his full-time role. During the afternoons and evenings he is out at sea in his fishing boat.

On top of all that, for three days a week he is selling fish from his shop in Perelle – much of which he has caught himself.

As an island we are not short of fresh fish outlets but I need to be sure that the fish I buy is locally caught and not imported. Dobbo is a neighbour and I know that the fish is from Guernsey waters and is as fresh as it can be – sometimes taking just a few hours to come from the sea to his shop where he prepares everything himself. It is a freshness you can taste.

As with anything, the supply is partially seasonal but Guernsey whiting, pollock, sea bass, mullet and mackerel are available throughout the year. All are relatively inexpensive and much under-rated… by everyone that is but Guernsey folk, who know how delicious they can be especially when cooked with fresh Guernsey herbs and locally-produced vegetables. I know too that I can get fresh skate, monkfish and crab, all of which are very popular at The Pavilion.

"I was born and bred in Guernsey and have always lived near the sea," said Dobbo, who has delivered post on the island for more than 20 years. "As children we lived on the beach. I went to sea almost before I could walk and was out on the boat fishing regularly with my father from the age of eight, but fishing has always been a precarious industry and not one on which to totally rely upon nowadays.

"When I was a youngster, full-time fishermen worked about 70 crab pots catching mainly crayfish. I've seen as many as 85 or 90 crayfish in a day from those crab pots. There are no full-time fishermen in Perelle now.

"I work about 40 pots in the summer, catching lobster, spider crab, mackerel and chancre or spider crab. In the winter it's more grille netting or line fishing for red mullet and sea bass. Anything I can't catch myself I buy from local fishermen".

LOBSTER SALAD WITH NEW SEASON POTATOES, GUERNSEY HERBS AND FENNEL

Serves 6

INGREDIENTS:

3x750g	Live lobsters
2 litres	Fish stock (see page 191)
100g	Mixed Guernsey salad leaves
3	Ripe tomatoes (blanched)
600g	New season potatoes
6	Free range eggs (soft boiled)
20g	Fresh Guernsey tarragon leaves
20g	Fresh Guernsey chives (chopped)
20g	Fresh Guernsey mint
200ml	Mayonnaise (see page 194)
10g	Caster sugar
	Sea salt
	Freshly ground black pepper

METHOD:

Heat the fish stock in a large saucepan and bring to the boil. Place the lobsters in the water and cook for 10-12 minutes on a rolling boil. Remove from the liquid and place in a sink of cold water.

Once cool, remove from the water and drain. Then remove the claws and crack using either a mallet or the back of a large cook's knife, carefully extracting the flesh and keeping the claws intact. Using a pair of kitchen scissors or sharp knife, cut along the line on the back of the lobster, cutting the shell in half. Remove the tail and make a slight incision along the back to remove the entrail line, which should be discarded.

Reserve any shell for use in other dishes such as Lobster Bisque.

Set aside the lobster meat in a refrigerator until required.

Wash and scrub the potatoes, then gently simmer in water together with the mint, caster sugar and a little salt until tender.

In a separate saucepan, boil some water, score the tomatoes with a sharp knife and add to the boiling water for 10 seconds. Remove and place immediately in cold water – this blanching process enables the skins to be removed easily. Slice the tomatoes and season with salt and pepper.

Blanch the tarragon in the same water for a couple of seconds before chopping and mixing with the mayonnaise.

Finally, boil the free range eggs in the same saucepan for 3 minutes until soft-boiled. Remove from the water and cool before peeling.

Serve the lobsters together with the tomato salad and soft-boiled eggs tossed in tarragon mayonnaise. Serve with fennel salad (see page 54), mixed Guernsey salad leaves and hot new potatoes sprinkled with chopped chives.

Tony Leck's Pavilion on a Plate

FRESHLY PICKED GUERNSEY CRAB SALAD WITH RED BELL PEPPER MAYONNAISE, SCORCHED CHERRY TOMATOES AND PARMESAN CRISPS

Serves 4 as a main course or 8 as a starter

This is a firm family favourite dish featured regularly upon our menu at the 'Pavilion'. The secret is to use seasonal produce at its best simply with minimal fuss, ideal for re-creating at home for friends and family.

METHOD:

Ask your fishmonger or supermarket for freshly-picked crab meat, but pick through the meat yourself to ensure any traces of shell are removed. Season the white crab meat with freshly ground pepper and a little sea salt, mix with a splash of lime juice and divide into four equal amounts ready for serving. Place in pastry rings or round pastry cutters of equal size and set aside in the refrigerator until required.

Using a pastry scraper, force the brown crab meat through a fine sieve and set aside.

To skin the tomatoes, firstly remove the core with a sharp knife, then make a small cross-shaped incision on the

INGREDIENTS:

750g	White crab meat
250g	Brown crab meat
1	Red bell pepper (peeled and puréed)
100ml	Mayonnaise
12	Cherry tomatoes
50g	Parmesan cheese (grated)
1	Tomato (skinned, flesh cut into dice)
3 tsp	Balsamic glaze
	Sea salt
	Freshly ground pepper
	Lime juice (splash)
	Extra virgin olive oil (splash)
	Seasonal fresh Guernsey herbs to accompany – chives, parsley, chervil and basil

other end of the tomato. Immerse each tomato in rapid boiling water for 10 seconds before removing and plunging into cold water. The skin should be easily removable. Remove the seeds and dice the flesh.

Meanwhile, place a red pepper into a hot oven for 10 minutes. Remove and immediately place in a plastic bag. This will sweat the pepper and help release the skin. Allow to cool before removing the unwanted skin and seeds. Purée the flesh of the pepper in a liquidiser with a little mayonnaise and season to taste.

To prepare parmesan crisps, simply sprinkle grated parmesan cheese on greaseproof paper and place in a moderate oven for ten minutes or until golden in colour. Remove from the baking sheet carefully and set aside.

Place each ring of white crab meat on a plate, top with a little brown crab meat and remove the pastry ring.

To serve, heat a non-stick pan until almost smoking. Add the cherry tomatoes and season with sea salt and fresh ground pepper. Allow the tomatoes to 'scorch' and blister. Finally add a splash of balsamic glaze and a little extra olive oil to enhance the flavour of the warm tomatoes.

Serve immediately with the chilled white and brown crab meat, red pepper mayonnaise and a mini salad of herbs and chopped tomato. Top with the parmesan crisps.

LOBSTER THERMIDOR

Serves 6

INGREDIENTS:

3x750g	Live lobsters
2 litres	Fish stock (see page 191)
1	Onion
1	Bay leaf
6	Black peppercorns
250ml	Guernsey Dairy milk
40g	Guernsey Dairy butter
30g	Plain flour
25ml	Brandy
1 tsp	English mustard
1	Clove of garlic (chopped)
40g	Fresh Guernsey tarragon leaves
75g	Guernsey Dairy mature cheddar
	Sea salt

METHOD:

Heat the fish stock in a large saucepan and bring to the boil then add the live lobsters and cook for 8-10 minutes on a rolling boil. Remove the lobsters from the liquid and place in a sink of cold water.

Once cool, remove from the water and drain. Take off the claws and crack using either a mallet or the back of a large cook's knife, carefully removing the flesh and keeping the claws intact. With a sharp knife, cut along the line which extends the length of the lobster's back and tail, cutting the shell in half lengthways. Take out the two halves of tail meat. Remove and discard the entrail line. Remove all meat from the shell. Separate the dark meat (and coral in female lobsters) from the white meat and reserve the half shell for serving.

Dice the lobster meat into 2cm pieces and refrigerate until required.

Prepare the sauce by putting the bay leaf, onion and peppercorns in a saucepan with the milk. Bring to boiling point and simmer for 2 minutes before removing from the heat. Set aside for the flavours to infuse for 10-12 minutes.

In a separate saucepan gently melt 20g of the butter over a medium heat, slowly adding the sieved flour. Cook as for a roux or until it becomes a thick paste. Add to this the infused milk little by little, stirring all the time to eliminate any lumps forming in the sauce. Cook over a low heat until the flour has been absorbed and the sauce has thickened. Stir in the mustard and pour the sauce through a sieve.

In a separate pan, gently melt the rest of the butter together with the chopped garlic. Add the diced lobster meat and coat with the butter. Pour onto this the brandy and ignite to burn off the alcohol. Pour the sauce onto the lobster. Fold in the chopped tarragon and season to taste.

Put the mixture back in shells and sprinkle with grated mature cheddar and place under a hot grill for 1-2 minutes until golden on top, ready to serve.

FISHERMAN'S SCOTCH EGGS

Serves 6

INGREDIENTS:

450g	Mashed potatoes
350g	Handpicked white crab meat
100g	Brown crab meat (sieved)
6	Scallops
1	Free range egg yolk
25g	Guernsey butter
5ml	Worcestershire sauce
10ml	Lobster or crab bisque (see page 34)
1	Spring onion (finely chopped)
5g	Stem ginger (finely chopped)
5g	Anchovy fillets (finely chopped)
	Sea salt
	Freshly ground pepper
	Flour, eggs and breadcrumbs to coat

METHOD:

Prepare mashed potatoes and pass through a fine sieve. Sauté chopped spring onion and ginger. Stir in Worcestershire sauce and chopped anchovies and mix with potatoes. Add to this the butter, bisque and egg yolk. Cook out over a low heat to dry out the potato.

Pick through the white crab meat to ensure there are no pieces of shell. Pass the brown crab meat through a fine sieve. Allow the potato mix to cool before adding the crab meat.

Prepare and clean the scallops. Remove the roe, slice finely and add to the potato mix. Season well with sea salt and freshly ground pepper. Place spoons of the potato mix into pastry rings or cutters, placing a raw scallop into the centre of each, and top with more potato. Shape into spheres and set aside in the refrigerator. Chill well before coating in a traditional pané of flour, eggs and breadcrumbs.

Deep fry in clean oil for 2 minutes before placing in a hot oven at 190°C, 375°F or Gas 5 for 8-9 minutes.

Ensure scallop is just cooked (medium rare) by inserting a skewer or probe into the centre.

To serve, place the fisherman's scotch eggs on some kitchen paper to drain and absorb any excess fat. Serve with a little salad, asparagus spears and chopped tomato with hollandaise sauce or lemony mayonnaise.

SEARED GUERNSEY SCALLOPS, BLACK PUDDING BONBONS WITH GREEN PEA PURÉE

Serves 6

METHOD:

Cut the black pudding into 2cm pieces and blitz in a blender for 30 seconds with a little beaten egg white. Roll the pudding into spheres approx. 30mm in diameter. Coat the spheres in seasoned flour, then dip in beaten egg. Finally roll in fine dried breadcrumbs and set aside in the refrigerator.

Slowly grill the bacon and cut them into triangular strips. Keep hot or reheat when ready to use.

When ready to serve, deep fry the black pudding bonbons until golden. Place on kitchen paper to absorb any excess oil and then put in a warm place or the bottom shelf of an oven.

Sauté the onion in a little butter until translucent. Add the bag of peas, cover with water from a boiling kettle and boil for a minute. Stir in freshly picked mint leaves and liquidise before passing the sauce through a fine sieve.

Season with salt and pepper.

Set the green sauce aside until ready to serve.

Brush each scallop with a little olive oil and sprinkle with sea salt. Place into a hot non-stick pan and cook for 30-45 seconds before turning the scallops over. Cook for a further 45-60 seconds before serving.

Remember, if too many scallops are placed into one pan this will reduce the required heat, so use two or more pans when cooking for larger numbers.

To serve, present the scallops on plates together with the black pudding bonbons, spoon around the green pea purée and add a crispy piece of bacon before serving.

A good supermarket or quality fishmonger will remove the scallops from their shells for you as well as the skirt and roe on request.

INGREDIENTS:

30	Scallops
250g	'Horseshoe' black pudding
125g	Bag frozen peas (de-frosted)
20g	Fresh Guernsey mint
50g	Chopped onion
30g	Unsalted Guernsey butter

6	Rashers streaky bacon
2	Free range eggs
	Plain flour (sieved)
	Fine dry breadcrumbs
	Sea salt
	Freshly ground black pepper
	Olive oil

ROAST BRILL FILLET
WITH WILD MUSHROOM 'VRAIC'

Serves 6

INGREDIENTS:

1100g	Brill (filleted)
650g	Wild mushrooms
125g	Shallots (finely chopped)
450g	Asparagus spears (peeled)
30g	Guernsey Dairy butter
125ml	Beef stock (see page 188)
125ml	Red wine
30g	Guernsey Dairy butter (ice cold and diced)
	Sea salt
	Freshly ground black pepper
15ml	Olive oil

METHOD:

Look for a whole brill approximately 2kg in weight and ask your fishmonger to divide it into 4 fillets, from which 6 equally sized portions can be cut. Keep the bones for use in other dishes.

Wash the fillets and carefully pat dry. Season with sea salt and a little pepper. Brush each fillet with a light stroke of olive oil. Heat a non-stick frying pan and place each fillet skin side down into the pan. Allow the skin to caramelise until a light golden colour, use a palette knife and turn each fillet over. Place the pan into a preheated oven 230°C, 450°F or Gas 8 for 6-8 minutes.

Sauté the chopped shallots in the butter until softened and translucent. Add the washed and patted-dried wild mushrooms, lightly sauté for

1-2 minutes, season with sea salt and pepper. Tip the shallots and mushrooms into a colander to drain.

Bring the red wine to boiling point and simmer until reduced in volume by half. Add the stock and reduce further until the sauce begins to thicken slightly. Add the reserved mushrooms and shallots. Remove from the heat source and whisk in the diced iced butter to thicken and enrich the sauce.

Place the asparagus spears into a saucepan of salted boiling water and cook until tender. Remove the spears with a slotted spoon and keep hot.

To serve

Divide and spoon the wild mushroom 'Vraic' onto your chosen serving plates. Remove the brill fillets from the oven and place on the mushrooms. Divide the hot asparagus between the plates and serve immediately.

The word 'Vraic' is used in the description of this dish to represent the likeness of seaweed washed-up on the beach. 'Vraic' is the Channel Island name given to seaweed, traditionally collected from the beaches and used as manure. The main use of Vraic is for spreading over potato fields during the winter months. It was then ploughed in to enrich the soil before the potatoes were planted in late winter and spring.

Gathering of 'Vraic' or Vraicking was an integral part of Island life in centuries gone by, with each Island parish allocated particular beaches where farmers and parishioners were allowed to collect or gather the seaweed. St. Andrews parishioners – the Island's only parish without any coastline – had the right to collect from Lihou Island and St Saviours area. Many farms had areas of land near the shoreline known as Secages – areas where the Vraic was spread out to dry. When excess amounts were collected it was then burnt, and the ashes used as winter fuel. Rich in iodine and potash, these ashes were ploughed into the soil.

SKATE WING (OFF THE BONE) WITH CAPER MASH, PARSLEY AND BEETROOT LEMON BUTTER

Serves 6

INGREDIENTS:

1	Large skate wing, skinned both sides, flesh removed from the bone/cartilage.
1kg	Maris Piper potatoes (prepared as for mashed potatoes)
450g	Guernsey butter
200ml	Guernsey cream
250g	Beetroot (cooked)
1 bunch	Flat leaf parsley
75g	Superfine capers
300g	Spinach
1 clove	Garlic
1	Shallot (chopped)
	Sea salt
	Freshly ground black pepper
	Olive oil

METHOD:

Trim the skate of any bits of cartilage or veins and divide the meat into six equal portions. The flesh can be folded over to ensure each portion is a similar size and thickness ensuring each portion will cook evenly.

Heat a non-stick saucepan until hot. Rub each portion of skate with a little olive oil and season well with salt and pepper. Place in pan and allow to caramelise slightly before turning each portion over. Place the pan in hot oven approx. 250°C, 485°F or Gas 9 for 7-8 minutes.

Meanwhile beat the mashed potatoes with 250g of the butter and all the cream. Add the capers and set aside to keep hot ready for serving.

Sauté the chopped shallot in a little butter before adding the spinach and cook with seasoning until just wilted.

Remove the skate from the oven and place each portion on a plate with some spinach and caper mash.

Using the same non-stick saucepan, melt the remaining butter and add to this the diced beetroot and chopped parsley. Squeeze in the juice of one lemon and check seasoning before serving with the beetroot lemon butter over the skate wing.

MUSSELS WITH ROCQUETTE CIDER, GUERNSEY CREAM AND CORIANDER

Serves 4

INGREDIENTS:

2kg	Mussels
150ml	Guernsey Dairy whipping cream
250ml	Rocquette cider
6	Shallots (finely diced)
1	Garlic clove (crushed)
25g	Fresh Guernsey parsley
75g	Fresh Guernsey coriander
25ml	Olive oil
10g	Chopped chilli (optional)
	Sea Salt
	Freshly ground white pepper

METHOD:

Scrub mussels under running water, removing the beard and scraping off any barnacles. Ensure the mussels are closed. Discard any that are broken or open. Drain the mussels in a colander, cover with a cool damp cloth and reserve in the refrigerator until required.

Heat the Rocquette cider in a separate saucepan and set aside keeping it hot.

To cook the mussels heat a large heavy-based saucepan on a high heat. Add the olive oil, diced shallots and crushed garlic. Stir for a few seconds before adding the mussels and hot cider. Ensure the shallots are evenly dispersed. Place a tight-fitting lid on the saucepan. Increase the heat and cook for approximately 3 minutes, giving the saucepan an occasional shake. When they have opened, remove from the saucepan with a spoon or pour through a sieve and place in serving bowls. Return the cider liquid to the heat, add the cream and boil rapidly to reduce for the accompanying sauce. While this is reducing check all the mussels have opened. If any have not, discard them immediately. Add finely chopped chilli at this stage if desired, followed by freshly picked and chopped coriander leaves and parsley. Serve immediately with fresh bread or Guernsey biscuits and Guernsey butter.

GUERNSEY SEA BASS FILLET, ROCQUETTE CIDER AND SEAFOOD MINESTRONE

Serves 6

INGREDIENTS:

1.2kg	Sea bass fillet
500g	Fish bones for stock
500ml	Rocquette dry cider
100ml	Dry white wine
150g	Courgettes
100g	Shallots
225g	Tomatoes
100g	Carrot
80g	Spaghetti (snipped)
100g	Palourdes or mussels
12	Scallops
100g	Queen scallops
100g	White crab meat
20g	Tarragon
20g	Chives
1	Clove garlic
1	Fennel bulb
50g	Guernsey butter
	Olive oil
	Sea salt
	Freshly ground pepper
	Parmesan cheese

METHOD:

To prepare a fish stock, first rinse the fish bones in plenty of cold water. Heat the olive oil in a large saucepan. Add the garlic, half of the chopped shallots and half of the fennel bulb and fry for 5 minutes without colouring. Pick the herbs and add the stalks to the pan along with the white wine. Increase the heat until boiling and reduce the liquid by half. Place the fish bones in the pan together with about one litre of water. Bring to the boil and skim any scum from the surface. Reduce heat and simmer gently for 20 minutes before straining through a

fine sieve. For a clearer stock pass through a fine muslin cloth again. Allow to cool. Refrigerate until required.

To prepare the minestrone, heat some olive oil in a large saucepan, add diced shallots, carrot, fennel and cook gently for 5 minutes until soft. Add the reduced fish stock and cider, bring to boiling point then drop in the snipped pasta. Cook until tender before adding the diced courgettes, cherry tomatoes and chopped herbs. Add the palourdes, freshly-picked crab meat and queen scallops, season to taste and set aside ready to serve.

Season the sea bass fillets on both sides and seal in a hot non-stick pan skin side down. When it is beginning to colour, turn each fillet over and place the pan in a hot oven for 5-6 minutes.

Season the scallops and sear in a separate non-stick pan and combine with the seafood minestrone broth.

Serve the broth in large bowls with a portion of sea bass and seared scallops. Finally, shave a little parmesan cheese on the top prior to serving.

MACKEREL FILLETS WITH GOOSEBERRIES

Serves 4

INGREDIENTS:

6	Medium mackerel
100g	Guernsey Dairy butter
400g	Fresh gooseberries
20g	Fresh mint (shredded)
30g	Caster sugar
20g	Fresh parsley (chopped)
	Sea salt
	Freshly ground black pepper

METHOD:

Fillet the mackerel and remove the 'pin-bones' from each fillet. This is easily done with a sharp cook's knife. Simply cut each side of where the 'pin-bones' are but do not cut through the skin. Then pull away the flesh. Score the thicker end of each fillet with a couple of slashes to enable even cooking. A fishmonger will also prepare this for you.

Wash each fillet and pat dry.

Trim the gooseberries by removing the 'tops 'n' tails' with a small knife before washing and patting dry.

Melt approximately 50g of Guernsey butter in a non-stick frying pan (or two – don't crowd the pan) and add the fillets.

Season with salt and pepper, turning the fillets over after 2-3 minutes. Remove each fillet and place upon a baking tray in a low oven, 160°C, 325°F or Gas 3 for 4-5 minutes.

Meanwhile add the prepared gooseberries to the same frying pan/s together with the remaining butter and sugar. Cook slowly for about 5 minutes until the gooseberries begin to 'give' or soften. Add the finely shredded fresh mint and stir carefully.

Remove the mackerel fillets from the oven and transfer to plates. Spoon over the gooseberries and any cooking liquor. Sprinkle with freshly chopped parsley and serve with hot new potatoes.

Mackerel, with its oily texture, combines well with the tartness of gooseberries. Try the same dish with rhubarb during earlier months of the year before gooseberries are readily available.

POACHED HADDOCK, BABY SPINACH RISOTTO, HOLLANDAISE SAUCE & POACHED FREE RANGE EGG

Serves 4

INGREDIENTS:

700g	White smoked haddock fillet (4 x 175g portions)
125g	Chopped onion
280g	Arborio risotto rice
500ml	Guernsey Dairy milk
250ml	Fish stock (see page 191)
300ml	Dry white wine
175g	Fresh Guernsey baby spinach
35g	Parmesan cheese
25ml	Olive oil
	Freshly ground black pepper
	Unbleached course sea salt

Poached eggs:

4	Free range eggs
	Splash white wine vinegar
	Hollandaise recipe (See page 195)

METHOD:

Cut the haddock fillets into four equal portions, remove any scales and any fine little 'pin-like' bones.

Wash and place in a heavy-based saucepan with the milk. Season with salt and pepper. Poach the fish over a low heat.

Finely chop the onion and place in a heavy-based saucepan with the olive oil over a medium heat. Stir constantly while adding the rice. Keep stirring until the onion becomes soft and translucent. Add the dry white wine a little at a time, constantly stirring with a spatula. Once all the wine is incorporated, start to add the fish stock a little at a time, allowing the rice to absorb the liquid whilst still stirring. Pour in some of the milk from the poached haddock if required to adjust the consistency. This will take about 20 minutes until the rice is 'al dente' or just cooked, still with a little bite.

As soon as the rice has reached this stage, take the rinsed baby spinach leaves and remove from the heat. Let the risotto stand for 3-4 minutes. Stir to incorporate all the ingredients. Finish with the parmesan and serve in bowls.

Poach the eggs in water seasoned with salt, pepper and white wine vinegar.

Drain the haddock fillets and place on the risotto, drain the poached eggs on kitchen paper and position on the haddock fillets.

Spoon a generous amount of Hollandaise sauce over the eggs and place under the grill for 15-20 seconds prior to serving.

1. Freshly gathered ormers in their shells.

2. Scrub the skirt to remove any grit.

3. To remove the ormer from its shell, cut away the fibrous pad.

4. Clean and pat dry the ormer.

5. Place between two cloths to protect the delicate flesh.

6. Beat with a mallet to help tenderise the ormer.

Tony Leck's Pavilion on a Plate

ORMERS

Ormers are considered a delicacy in the Channel Islands. They are part of the family which includes the abalone and are found in places as diverse as Japan, California and Australia. The Bailiwick of Guernsey is their most northerly European location. The word ormer derives from 'orielle de mer' or 'ear of the sea' due to its shape.

Ormers thrive on certain varieties of seaweed and live in rugged areas of the sea, clinging to large rocks often only accessible during certain low tides. Due to the dramatic depletion in recent years of their numbers, the gathering of ormers is now restricted to a number of 'ormering tides' in any given year – namely, the days of the full moon, the new moon and the two days following between January 1st and April 30th. Strict regulations are in place to ensure gatherers do not remove ormers under the minimum size of 8cm along the longest axis of the shell. Whilst gathering these fruits of the sea, no diving apparatus such as snorkels, flippers etc. are allowed and any breach of the law can result in a heavy fine or term of imprisonment.

The quest for ormers even led to Britain's first ever underwater arrest, which saw a gatherer caught illegally diving for the shellfish in full diving gear. Similarly, ormers are not allowed to be bought or sold on any day other than those specifically permitted. This does not apply to preserved ormers – that is one that has been cooked or pickled, but not one that has been deep frozen.

TRADITIONAL GUERNSEY ORMER CASSEROLE

Serves 4 - Allow two or three ormers per person, depending upon size of ormer and how hearty you wish to make the dish.

INGREDIENTS:

8-12	Ormers
6	Shallots or 1 large onion
400g	Carrots
2	Bay leaves
150g	Belly pork or bacon
150g	Guernsey Dairy butter
	Salt and pepper
	Flour for dusting
500ml	Guernsey ale

METHOD:

Preparation:

Soak the ormers in fresh cold water for at least 1 hour. Extract from their shells by laying the ormer shell side down in the palm of your hand and slipping a knife around under the fibrous muscle in the centre which attaches to the shell. Use a glove or some other protection for your hand and gently ease the ormer from its shell. Use a small nail brush to scrub the flesh and frilly skirt to remove any grit. Once thoroughly scrubbed and rinsed, pat dry with a cloth, place each ormer between a cloth and beat with a rolling pin or butchers mallet to help tenderise the flesh. Do not over-pulverise the flesh as this might break the ormers into pieces.

Cooking Method:

Season the flour with salt and pepper and lay the ormers into the flour on both sides.

Melt the butter in a frying pan and gently fry the ormers until golden brown on both sides.

Transfer to a casserole dish.

Dice the belly pork or bacon and fry off in the frying pan together with the diced carrot and onion. Add to the casserole dish with the bay leaves. Pour in the ale, heat gently and place in a pre-heated oven at 160-170°C under a tight fitting lid for 2 hours. Reduce the oven temperature and allow the casserole to cook gently until the ormers are tender.

Whilst this is in the oven prepare some mashed potato to serve as a traditional accompaniment.

GUERNSEY CHANCRE CRAB AND FRESH GUERNSEY HERB CAKES WITH CHILLI DRESSING

Serves 4 (8 as a starter)

INGREDIENTS:

400g	New potatoes
250g	White crabmeat
200g	Brown crabmeat
15g	Chopped parsley
15g	Chopped chives
30g	Chopped coriander
30g	Chopped basil
10g	Tomato ketchup
	Sea salt
	Freshly ground pepper

Traditional pané mix:

100g	Breadcrumbs
100g	Plain flour
250ml	Guernsey milk
1	Free range egg

Chilli Dressing:

1	Fresh chilli pepper
375ml	Rice vinegar
125g	Granulated sugar
1	Lime (juiced)

METHOD:

Wash the new potatoes and simmer gently in seasoned water until tender. Remove from heat and refresh under cold water. Drain the potatoes well and lightly crush with a fork. Set aside.

Pass the brown crabmeat through a fine mesh sieve to remove any traces of shell. Pick through the white crabmeat and remove any shell.

Bind together the crushed new potatoes, brown and white crabmeat, tomato ketchup and chopped fresh Guernsey herbs. Season with salt and pepper to taste.

Divide the mixture into eight pattie shapes or spoon into a 7cm diameter pastry ring and repeat until all the mixture is used.

Place in a refrigerator until firm.

Once the crab cakes are firm, coat them with seasoned plain flour. Dip each one in a mixture of beaten egg and milk. Finally roll in fine breadcrumbs, re-shape with a palette knife to make the cakes uniform.

Gently fry each cake in a generous amount of Guernsey butter, turning each over as necessary. Heat through in a moderate oven before serving with chilli dressing and a salad of fresh Guernsey herbs.

For the chilli dressing:

Finely chop the chilli pepper and add to the rice vinegar and sugar in a saucepan over a medium heat. Stir to dissolve the sugar and simmer for 15 minutes or until mixture has reduced to a thin syrup. Remove from heat and add lime juice.

Serve with a salad of fresh Guernsey herbs.

CUTTLEFISH WITH INK RISOTTO AND CHORIZO

Serves 4 (8 as a starter)

INGREDIENTS:

600g	Cuttlefish
125g	Chopped onion
275g	Arborio risotto rice
700ml	Fish stock (see page 191)
250ml	Dry white wine
20g	Fresh Guernsey parsley
20g	Fresh Guernsey chives
50g	Parmesan cheese
25ml	Olive oil
25ml	Cuttlefish ink
75g	Chorizo sausage
	Freshly ground black pepper
	Unbleached course sea salt

METHOD:

Rinse the cuttlefish well in order to be able to see clearly whilst cleaning them. Remove the head from the body by pulling it away; cut the body open, carefully pull out the two silvery ink sacs and reserve for use in the risotto later.

Empty the body of its innards and pull the two wings away. If the fish is large then the skin will need to be removed, though on younger, smaller fish this isn't required. Wash the fish once again and slice the flesh into slithers approximately 2.5cm wide. When preparing the head beware as the upper part contains a lot of the inky liquid. Discard the round protruding beak first, then cut along under the eyes, thus separating the tentacles which are attached on a thin strip. Discard the eyes. Separate the tentacle into four smaller bunches.

Finely chop the onion and place in a heavy-based saucepan with the olive oil over a medium heat. Stir constantly adding the rice; keep stirring until the onion becomes soft and translucent. Add the dry white wine a little at a time, constantly stirring with a spatula. Once all the wine is incorporated add the fish stock a little at a time, allowing the rice to absorb the liquid whilst still stirring. This will take approximately 20 minutes until the rice is 'al dente' or just cooked, still with a little bite. As soon as the rice has reached this stage, remove from the direct source of heat; let the risotto stand for 3-4 minutes.

Stir the risotto to incorporate all the ingredients including the chopped parsley and finely-chopped chives; spoon into bowls.

Sauté the strips of cuttlefish in a splash of olive oil and season generously, reduce heat and cook until tender, add diced chorizo sausage and continue to sauté until cooked.

Add grated parmesan cheese to the risotto and stir before dividing equal portions into serving bowls. Dress the serving dishes with the cuttlefish mixture and serve.

CHANCRE CRAB RISOTTO
WITH GUERNSEY HERB SALAD

Serves 4 (8 as a starter)

INGREDIENTS:

400g	White crabmeat
250g	Brown crabmeat
125g	Chopped onion
280g	Arborio risotto rice
600ml	Fish stock (see page 191)
350ml	Dry white wine
25g	Fresh Guernsey chives
100g	Mascarpone cheese
25ml	Olive oil
	Freshly ground black pepper
	Unbleached course sea salt

Salad

50g	Fresh Guernsey basil leaves
25g	Fresh Guernsey chervil
25g	Fresh Guernsey chives
25g	Parmesan cheese
	Olive oil
	Balsamic glaze

METHOD:

Finely chop the onion and place in a heavy-based saucepan with the olive oil over a medium heat. Stir constantly, adding the rice a little at a time. Keep stirring until the onion becomes soft and translucent. Add the dry white wine a little at a time, constantly stirring with a spatula. Once all the wine is incorporated, start to stir in the fish stock a little at a time, allowing the rice to absorb the liquid. Add the brown crabmeat towards the end of the cooking stage. This will take approximately 20 minutes until the rice is 'al dente' or just cooked, still with a little bite.

Add the mascarpone cheese and remove from the direct source of heat. Let the risotto stand for 3-4 minutes. Stir the risotto to incorporate all the ingredients, adding the white crabmeat and finely chopped chives. Serve in bowls.

Toss the freshly-picked herbs together with a little olive oil and balsamic glaze. Season to taste before serving alongside the risotto with freshly shaved parmesan.

SALT 'N' PEPPER SQUID WITH CHILLI DRESSING AND SALAD

Serves 4 (8 as a starter)

INGREDIENTS:

1.1kg	Squid (cleaned)
25g	Black peppercorns
25g	Sichuan peppercorns
25g	Unbleached coarse sea salt
1	Chilli pepper (finely chopped)
25ml	Olive oil

Dressing:

1	Chilli pepper (finely chopped)
375ml	Rice vinegar
125g	Granulated sugar
1	Lime

Salad:

1	Sweet red pepper
1	Green pepper
1	Red onion
3	Spring onions (finely chopped)
½	Cucumber
50g	Fresh Guernsey basil leaves
75g	Fresh Guernsey coriander
25g	Fresh Guernsey chives
25ml	Sesame oil
10ml	Dark soy sauce
	Pinch caster sugar
	Pinch salt

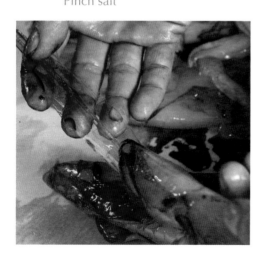

METHOD:

To make the dressing, cut the chilli pepper in half lengthwise. Remove seeds and finely chop. Place the rice vinegar, sugar and chilli pepper in a saucepan over a medium heat. Stir to dissolve the sugar. Once at boiling point, reduce heat. Allow to simmer for 15 minutes or until the mixture has reduced to a thin syrup. Remove from heat and add the juice of one lime. Pour through a sieve and set aside.

For the salad, peel and de-seed the cucumber and slice into thin strips. Slice the peppers and red onion into similar-sized thin strips. Toss together with the sesame oil and dark soy sauce; sprinkle over the salad a pinch each of caster sugar and salt. Set aside in a large bowl. Pick the herbs and set aside.

To clean the squid, gently pull apart the head and body. The intestines will come out with the head and are joined to the tentacles.

Using a knife, remove the tentacles and cut into bite-size pieces. Place your fingers into the body and remove the remaining insides together with the 'see through' plastic-like quill. Try to remove the ink sac without piercing it, so this can be reserved for use in alternative dishes. Remove the two fins from the side of the tube and reserve with the tentacles. Discard the quill and intestines. Cut along the faint marking line on one side of the tube to create a large rectangle of flesh. Remove any white roe and fine membrane using a sharp knife. Score the flesh on the outside in a crisscross pattern. Clean the flesh under cold running water and pat dry. Cut into four equal portions.

To serve, rub the Sichuan pepper, coarse sea salt, finely chopped chillies and cracked peppercorns with olive oil into the flesh. Heat a non-stick pan and fry each piece for no more than 2 minutes, turning over midway. In a wok, stir fry the salad, adding the picked herbs at the last minute. Serve the squid on the salad. Reheat the chilli dressing and drizzle around the salad.

C.L.T.
OUR VERSION OF THE FAMOUS B.L.T.
ONLY MADE WITH FRESH GUERNSEY CHANCRE CRAB!
Serves 6

Served with red bell-pepper mayonnaise, cherry tomatoes, shaved Parmesan cheese and a mini salad of freshly picked herbs.

INGREDIENTS:

500g	Freshly picked white crabmeat
500g	Brown crabmeat
100ml	Red bell pepper mayonnaise (See page 194)
3	Plum tomatoes (skinned and cut into halves)
18	Cherry tomatoes
20ml	Balsamic vinegar
6	Homemade bread rolls or mini loaves
	Sea salt & freshly ground black peppercorns.
	Splash of lime or lemon juice
	Rocket salad leaves
	Freshly-picked basil

METHOD:

Simply use freshly-picked crabmeat, season with freshly ground pepper and a little sea salt. Mix with a splash of lime or lemon juice and bind with a little red bell pepper mayonnaise. Divide into six equal amounts and sandwich within home made bread with rocket salad and halved plum tomatoes.

Spread a generous coating of brown crabmeat over the top of the sandwich and serve with freshly picked basil leaves and cherry tomatoes.

FISH IN BEER BATTER

Serves 6-8

INGREDIENTS:

6-8x175g   Cod fillets
            (skinned and bones removed)
            (alternatively use plaice,
            haddock, whiting or pollack)

            Sea salt

            Freshly ground black pepper.

            Oil for deep-frying

Traditional beer batter

450ml   Favourite beer

300g   Plain flour

1 tsp   Salt

1 tsp   Caster sugar

20g   Fresh yeast

For a light beer batter

450ml   Favourite beer (ice cold)

330g   Self raising flour

1 tsp   Salt

METHOD:

To prepare the traditional beer batter, place the yeast and sugar in a large bowl and stir in approximately one third of the beer to create a paste. Sieve into this the flour and mix well with a whisk. Using the whisk, gradually add the remaining beer. Finally add the salt and leave the batter to 'rest' for about an hour before using.

For the light batter, sieve the flour and salt together into a large bowl and pour in the ice cold beer. Mix together quickly with a whisk.

Don't worry if the batter has one or more lumps in – these will separate from the fish when frying to give you batter scraps. Use this batter immediately.

Follow a few basic rules when frying fish. Firstly, use clean oil and lots of it. Each dish or component of a dish requires plenty of space or room in the deep fryer so as not to stick together. Also, so that the temperature does not drop, do not add too much to the oil at once. The choice of oil is yours – some prefer vegetable oil, sunflower oil or maybe even beef dripping.

Heat the oil to 180-190°C or 350-375°F, depending on the thickness of the cod fillets. Thicker chunks should be fried at a slightly lower temperature to ensure the fish cooks through without burning the outside of the batter.

Season the fillets of fish with salt and pepper. Dip each fillet into a light coating of plain flour and lightly shake to remove any excess. Then dip each fillet into the batter and carefully place into the hot oil and fry for approximately 6-8 minutes depending upon size. Turn each fillet over mid-way through to ensure even cooking.

Remove the fish from the fryer and place on a tray of kitchen paper to absorb any excess oil. Serve immediately or retain hot for several minutes by placing in a low temperature oven while you fry the remainder of the fish.

Serve with chips, mushy peas and tartare sauce.

GUERNSEY FRESH HERBS

Now, let your senses get to grips with some of these.

The intense aroma of mint… the unmistakable aniseed taste of fennel… and what would so many dishes be without parsley?

Next, imagine a greenhouse longer than a football pitch, carpeted with coriander, another filled with the sweet smell of basil… stadiums of freshness, stadiums of intense flavour.

For those who have never been – that's what it is like at Guernsey Fresh Herbs.

A visitor to the island asked me if herbs grown in Guernsey really are better than anywhere else – or is it just hype?

I can only give my opinion based on long experience in the kitchen. I've had plenty of opportunity to compare.

The ones grown locally are the best in the world. Why? Who knows? It could be something to do with the clean sea air or the soil, the warm climate and the mild winters. It could be because

I receive them so fresh – I can speak with the supplier at 9am and be using them in preparation before lunch service.

My passion for fresh ingredients is well-known around Guernsey, and herbs are no exception. They can transform the taste of a dish, or ruin it if they're not right.

One man who understands my insistence on the finest is Siegi Moherndl. His firm Guernsey Fresh Herbs started 25 years ago as a tomato grower. Their production of herbs started with a handful of pots but now commands over 20 acres. What I love about them is that despite their phenomenal success, they never stop being creative, trying new things, growing new products. Every time I visit, Siegi has a new variety to show me. For example, I'm still discovering new types of mint I never knew existed.

It comes as no surprise to me that they are an award-winning company and were recently named Guernsey Good Food Producer of the Year. It's not only local restaurants and hotels which prize Siegi's produce – it is available in most food retail outlets on the island and is exported to the length of the UK, from the south coast to Scotland.

I include Siegi among my personal friends as well as a supplier. We are near neighbours and frequent the same hostelry.

He came to the firm in 1989 to provide temporary holiday cover for one of the staff and he's been there ever since. Siegi was born on the island and followed his father into horticulture. He puts his success partly down to the fact his firm is a 'clean' producer. He uses steam sterilisation in place of chemicals and bugs are kept at bay using biological control – in other words bugs that eat other bugs.

The finished result speaks for itself. It is something the island can be proud of.

Tony Leck's Pavilion on a Plate

Tony Leck's Pavilion on a Plate

PORKY'S

Jason Hamon and Matthew Bateman grew up together on Guernsey. They went to the same school and both work at Forest Stores – Guernsey's premier independent food store - where I first met them.

Jason is a butcher by trade and Matt is the shop floor manager. I really got to know them when they began a company of their own, Porky's. As the name hints, they're in the business of high quality pork from pigs carefully reared on their own farm.

It began in 2008, when the two of them bought a field and started a pig farm as a small independent venture. The herd has now grown from the initial 14 to almost 80 today, spread over two fields in St Saviour's, just around the corner from The Pavilion.

"Our pork has a unique flavour which we think is achieved through feeding them pig nut and fresh apples, cabbages, lettuces and vegetables from the store where we both still work. We are also able to feed them with the apple pulp from the Rocquette cider farm," said Jason.

They rear a number of different breeds, each with its own appeal – Berkshire, Large White, Gloucester Old Spot, Oxford Sandy and Black – as well as others they have crossbred for a large eye in the chops and the right amount of fat.

"We pride ourselves on being free-range with animal welfare as a top priority," added Matt. All the pigs are individually named by Jason and Matt, who divide the work equally between the two families.

PAVILION'S TRADITIONAL GUERNSEY BEAN JAR

Serves 6

INGREDIENTS:

375g	Butter beans
375g	Haricot beans
250g	Onions (chopped)
250g	Carrots (chopped)
500ml	Good clear beef stock (see page 188)
20g	Guernsey Herbs fresh thyme
10g	Black peppercorns
2	Ham hocks or pig's trotters

METHOD:

Soak the haricot and butter beans overnight in a large container of cold water with the ham hocks.

Drain and refresh with more water and bring to the boil in a large saucepan.

Once at boiling point remove the beans and ham hocks and place in a large earthenware pot. Discard the water.

Add the chopped onions, carrots, picked thyme stalks and crushed peppercorns.

Pour onto this the beef stock, topping up with water if necessary. Heat gently and cover with a tight-fitting lid or seal with foil.

Place in a low to moderate oven at 150-170° C, 300-340°F or Gas 3-4 for between 4-5 hours, until the beans are tender and the meat falls away from the bone.

Before serving, remove the ham hocks or trotters. Separate the meat from the bones. Replace the meat and serve with freshly-baked Guernsey biscuits (see page 201) and plenty of butter.

SLOW-BRAISED SHANKS OF SARK LAMB, RED WINE SAUCE

Serves 6

INGREDIENTS:

6	Lamb shanks
6	Cloves garlic (peeled and sliced)
750ml	Bottle red wine
500ml	Lamb stock (see page 188)
6-8	Juniper berries
5-6	Bay leaves
3-4 tbsp	Red wine vinegar
100g	Sultanas
	Crushed black peppercorns
	Sea salt
2	Glasses of Port to taste

METHOD:

Cut deep incisions into the lamb shanks with a small sharp knife and insert a slice of garlic into each incision together with some sultanas. Season the shanks with sea salt and crushed peppercorns.

In a large container, place juniper berries, bay leaves, red wine vinegar, red wine and lamb stock.

Cover and refrigerate. Allow to marinade for 2-3 days. To ensure an even coating of marinade, turn the shanks at intervals, once or twice a day.

To braise the shanks, remove from the marinade and place in a hot frying pan to lightly brown and seal the meat. Heat the marinade gently in an ovenproof dish and return the lamb shanks. Seal the ovenproof dish and place in a medium oven. Cook for approximately 3 hours. Turn the shanks at regular intervals to ensure even cooking.

Do not rush this cooking time. If you prefer reduce the oven temperature slightly and cook the lamb slower. The shanks should be very tender, but still attached to the bone.

After cooking return the shanks to the oven on a roasting tray to crisp up the outer skin.

Sieve the cooking liquid into a saucepan. Bring to the boil, add the Port and reduce the liquid to your preferred sauce consistency.

Serve with minted new season potatoes in Spring and Summer, creamy mashed potatoes during Winter months or dauphinoise potatoes (see page 200).

Sark lamb has a unique flavour due to its grazing land. Imagine an Island without the pollution from cars or other vehicles, an island that is only 3 miles long and 1.5 miles wide where the only way to get around is on foot, bicycle or horse and cart. With the only engine-driven vehicles being tractors used for farming. The rugged coastline and open fields are licked with the wonderful sea breeze daily, giving the lambs a flavour similar to those reared on the salt marshes of Mont Saint Michel across the water in northern France.

Sark lamb tends to have a higher amount of fat compared to other lambs, but for me this is where the natural distinctive flavours exude.

MOUS'SARK'A

Serves 6

INGREDIENTS:

675g	Sark lamb (minced)
250g	Shallots (finely chopped)
3	Cloves of garlic (finely chopped)
400g	Fresh ripe tomatoes (diced small)
10g	Fresh Guernsey oregano
10g	Fresh Guernsey lemon thyme
10g	Fresh Guernsey mint (chopped)
2	Bay leaves
¼ tsp	Cinnamon powder
¼ tsp	Allspice powder
175ml	Dry white wine
75ml	Olive oil
2	Large jacket potatoes (peeled and thinly sliced)
4	Medium aubergines (cut into 1cm slices)
75g	Plain flour
	Sea salt
	Freshly ground black pepper

Topping:

75g	Guernsey Dairy butter
75g	Plain flour
800ml	Guernsey Dairy milk
200g	Parmesan cheese (grated)
1	Free range egg
2	Free range egg yolks

Salad:

6	Slices of crusty bread
250g	Ripe vine tomatoes (sliced)
125g	Cucumber (peeled and diced)
10g	Fresh Guernsey mint (shredded)
	Olive oil
	Malt vinegar
	Sea salt

METHOD:

Pre-heat the oven to 180°C, 350°F, Gas 4.

Heat the olive oil in a large saucepan or casserole dish and add the chopped shallots. Cook gently for 10 minutes until the shallots are soft and translucent, but not coloured. Place in a large colander to drain. Using the same saucepan or casserole dish, add the minced lamb and allow to brown, stirring occasionally with a spatula to break down any lumps. Cook until all the meat has a loose texture and is evenly browned. Place the meat into a large colander to drain any excess fat from the mixture.

Place the saucepan or casserole dish back onto the heat and deglaze by adding the dry white wine. Add the drained mince and shallots then the garlic, tomatoes, bay leaves, lemon thyme and oregano. Stir in the ground cinnamon and allspice. Heat to simmering point and cook gently, stirring occasionally, for approximately 1 hour, adding the chopped mint at the last moment.

Place the sliced aubergines into the colander, sprinkle liberally with sea salt, and leave for 30 minutes. This draws out any of the bitter juices in the aubergine.

Prepare the topping by melting the butter in a large heavy-based saucepan. Add 75g plain flour and stir. Gradually add the milk. Stir continuously until the sauce thickens and all the milk is incorporated. Simmer gently for a further 5 minutes before removing from the heat and stirring in half the grated parmesan cheese. Season with salt and pepper to taste. Allow to cool for 5-10 minutes before whisking the egg and egg yolks into the sauce.

Meanwhile, rinse the sliced aubergines in cold water and pat dry. Dust the dried slices with flour and fry each slice in batches in olive oil until golden on both sides. Place on kitchen paper to drain any excess oil.

To construct the dish, cover the base of a large casserole dish or earthenware pot with approximately one-third of the mince, then a layer of thinly-sliced potatoes followed by a layer of aubergine slices. Repeat the layers, ending with the top using the last of the mince. Pour on the prepared cheese sauce. Sprinkle the top with the remaining grated parmesan cheese and place in the pre-heated oven for 45-60 minutes or until the topping is golden and the cheese sauce is bubbling. Remove from the oven and allow to stand for 5 minutes before cutting into portions and serving.

Serve with a fresh salad of ripe vine tomatoes, diced cucumber and shredded mint served on slices of crusty bread and liberally seasoned with sea salt, olive oil and malt vinegar.

This dish cannot be beaten for a simple alfresco dinner party; made using locally-grown aubergines and freshly picked herbs, it is best eaten with a salad of freshly picked vine tomatoes and cucumber tossed in minted vinegar with a generous drizzle of olive oil and seasoning, together with a loaf of freshly baked crusty bread.

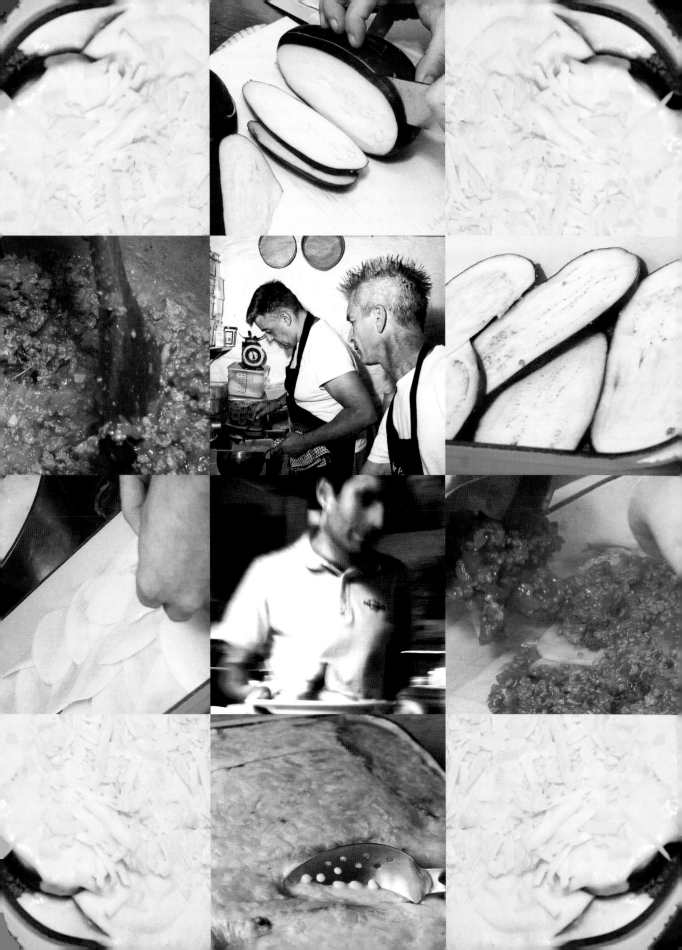

BOILED HAM WITH WHITE ONION SAUCE

Serves 6

INGREDIENTS:

1.5kg	Joint of boneless gammon
1	Large carrot
2	Sticks celery
1	Large onion
2	Medium leeks
2	Cooking apples
3	Whole cloves
	Pinch cinnamon
	Pinch nutmeg

White onion sauce:

150g	Onion (thinly sliced)
400ml	Guernsey Dairy milk
100ml	Guernsey Dairy cream
30g	Guernsey Dairy butter
30g	Plain flour
3	Whole cloves
	Salt
	Freshly-ground white pepper

Alternatively serve with a parsley sauce (see page 192)

METHOD:

To remove some of the saltiness of the gammon, soak the joint overnight in cold water, changing the water once or twice. The following day, cut the joint into two or three equal-sized pieces. Cover the work surface with several layers of clingwrap and roll up each cut of gammon into a sausage shape. Seal with another layer of clingwrap to hold their shape. Pierce each roll with several small indentations using a sharp pointed knife – this still allows the flavours to come through without the joints losing their shape.

Place in a large saucepan with the chopped celery, carrot, leeks, whole apples and onion. Cover with fresh water and bring to boil, skim any scum from the surface and continue to cook on a rolling simmer for up to 2 hours or until cooked. Ensure the joints are covered with water at all times when cooking. Remove the joints, place on a deep tray and allow to drain slightly. Using a small cook's or office knife remove the skin and set aside. Roll the ham again very tightly in clingwrap until it is a sausage shape and reserve in the refrigerator until required.

The excess skin can be dried into crackling by either placing in the bottom of a low oven to dry or by crisping up under a hot grill and used in other dishes.

Bear in mind the weight of the ham may now have reduced by up to a third. Retain the ham stock for use in other recipes.

The joints will firm up when cool and easily retain their shape, keeping well in the refrigerator for up to five days as they are thoroughly sealed.

For an alternative dish with a barbeque-style flavour, try boiling the gammon in a large saucepan of cola.

For the white onion sauce:

Slice the onion and sweat off in the Guernsey butter. Once the onion is translucent, sieve and retain the fat, adding the flour to make a white roux. Cook the roux without colour for 3-4 minutes, allow to cool.

Heat the Guernsey milk, infusing with the cloves and the cooked sliced onion.

Add this gradually to the white roux to make a white sauce.

Cook over a low heat for 25 minutes, stirring regularly.

Meanwhile, reheat the ham by cutting into thick slices and placing in a hot water bath in the oven, sealed with a tight fitting lid or a layer of kitchen foil until the ham is heated through. Once thoroughly heated through, check the seasoning of the sauce and serve.

SLOW-ROASTED BELLY PORK, APPLE MASH, BARBEQUED ROCQUETTE CIDER SAUCE

Serves 4

INGREDIENTS:

800-900g	Pork belly (scored)
250ml	Chicken or pork stock (see page 189)
500ml	Rocquette cider
100g	Onion (chopped)
100g	Leek (chopped)
100g	Carrot (chopped)
100g	Celery (chopped)
450g	Maris Piper potatoes
2	Medium Bramley apples
50ml	Barbeque sauce essence
	Olive oil
	Sea salt
	Black peppercorns
	Mustard seeds
	Lemon pepper
	Clove
	Lemon grass
	Chilli peppers

METHOD:

Score the pork belly skin if required and remove any bones. Trim any excess pieces of pork off which will later be used as lardons with the greens to accompany this dish.

Marinade the pork belly with the light spices – mustard seeds, lemon pepper, lemon grass, chilli peppers and a whole freshly ground clove and cider overnight.

Roughly chop the onion, leek, carrot and celery before browning off in a large heavy-based roasting tray, add the stock and the marinated pork. Bring to a simmer and cover before placing in a moderately hot oven to slow-roast for 3 hours at 150-170°C, 300-340°F or Gas 3-4.

Prepare potatoes for mash. Prepare apples for apple purée.

To serve:

Remove belly pork when tender, set aside and allow to rest.

Prepare sauce using the sticky residue and vegetables from slow-roasting pot, add the barbeque essence and simmer until required. Adjust seasoning and consistency of sauce.

Check consistency of mash and adjust with apple purée. Season to taste.

Carve the belly pork and reheat under a hot grill to crisp up the crackling, assemble components upon plates.

Re-check seasoning of sauce and serve.

POACHED LEG OF MUTTON
WITH CAPER SAUCE

Serves 8-10

INGREDIENTS:

2.5kg	Leg of mutton (boned & rolled)
1.5kg	Onions (peeled & sliced)
1 head	Celery (roughly chopped)
500g	Carrots (peeled & roughly chopped)
3-4	Whole cloves
1	Cinnamon stick (broken)
2	Cloves garlic (chopped)
2 litres	Chicken stock (see page 189)
	Salt
	Freshly cracked black peppercorns

Caper Sauce:

500ml	Mutton cooking liquor
500ml	Dry white wine
500ml	Guernsey Dairy cream
250g	Guernsey Dairy butter
200g	Plain flour
30g	Lilliput capers
50ml	Dry sherry
8	Anchovy fillets (drained and finely chopped)

METHOD:

Place the boned and rolled leg of mutton in a large pan of hot chicken stock. Add the various spices and chopped vegetables. Create a layer of sliced onions, then top up with hot water if required.

Ensure the mutton is covered, then bring to the boil and skim off any foam or crust that forms at the top of the pan. Allow the pan to simmer very gently for approximately 30 minutes for every 500g of meat or until tender.

For the Caper sauce:

Remove approximately 500ml of the cooking liquor from the pot and bring to boiling point in a separate saucepan. Stir in the white wine and boil again until reduced in volume by about a half. Add the cream and return to simmering.

Melt the butter in a third saucepan, adding the flour to create a roux.

Slowly add the simmering liquid as if you were making a white béchamel sauce.

When ready to serve, finish the sauce by adding the capers, dry sherry and chopped anchovies.

Remove the mutton from its cooking liquor and allow to rest before slicing. Serve with the chopped celery, carrot and sliced onions. Alternatively, serve with pickled red cabbage (see page 197).

Finally, pour over some of the caper sauce.

LOIN OF PORK WITH BAYEUX MUSTARD SAUCE

Serves 6

INGREDIENTS:

2kg	Pork loin joint
25g	Black peppercorns
45g	Unbleached coarse sea salt
2	Baking apples
1	Onion
1	Carrot
3	Sticks celery
250ml	Rocquette cider
25ml	Olive oil

Sauce:

450g	Pork bones (chopped) (ask your butcher to do this)
1	Carrot
1	Onion
2	Celery sticks
1	Bulb garlic
25g	Fresh Guernsey thyme
2	Baking apples
80g	Wholegrain Bayeux mustard
330ml	Rocquette cider
330ml	Brown chicken stock (see page 189)
75ml	Guernsey cream

METHOD:

Season the loin of pork well with the salt and pepper, taking care to rub the coarse sea salt in well to help crisp up the crackling later.

Heat a roasting tray in a hot oven or on the hob at a high temperature. Rub the oil onto the pork loin and place the meat in the roasting tray. Seal thoroughly by turning before adding chopped onion, carrot, celery and apple to the roasting tray. Allow the vegetables to caramelise slightly before adding the Rocquette cider.

Place in a pre-heated oven 200°C, 400°F, Gas 6 and roast for approximately 1½ hours.

Using a separate large, heavy-based saucepan, heat over high flame until hot and add the pork bones together with the remaining chopped vegetables, stir occasionally whilst allowing the bones and vegetables to caramelise.

Add the garlic and chopped apples (it's not necessary to peel or core the apples) followed by the Rocquette cider and chicken stock.

Bring to boiling point and, using a ladle, skim any impurities off the top; allow the stock to simmer for 1 hour.

Remove the loin from the oven and allow to rest in a warm place. Add the meat juices and vegetables to the sauce and reheat. Pass the sauce through a fine sieve and simmer until required consistency is reached. Add the wholegrain mustard to the sauce together with the Guernsey cream prior to serving.

Remove the crackling from the pork in one whole piece before carving. Portion the crackling and serve immediately with braised red cabbage (see page 196) and crisp roast potatoes.

MEADOW COURT FARM

Meadow Court Farm is one of my favourite places on Guernsey because it is home to the island's world-famous occupants – Golden Guernsey cattle. The breed's origins are buried in the mists of time but it is thought they stem from crossing native black wild cattle and larger cows from Italy, with a touch of Norse thrown into the mix at some stage. However it came about, the result has proved to be one of Guernsey's greatest assets – and one which I could not do without. The Guernsey cow not only produces some of the finest milk on the planet but also, in Ray Watts' capable hands, quality cuts of meat which taste unlike anything found anywhere else in the world.

Meadow Court Farm has been run by the Watts family since the 1970s. They have a strong commitment to the island as well as to maintaining the purity of the cattle.

At one time the farm focused on milk production but a few years ago quotas were imposed which changed Ray Watts' thinking. "To push the business forward we decided to supply meat as well as milk," he said. "It started in a small way and we found by producing beef our reputation spread across the island. What we do is very special and unique to Guernsey.

"Tony is one of our regulars. He prides himself on using local produce and has been a customer of ours for many years. Our working relationship has evolved into mutual respect."

Ray, who was brought up on a farm in Somerset, moved to the island more than 40 years ago and now, with his son James, has a well-established 130 strong milking herd and a small beef herd. "It took some getting used to at first – the small fields and very narrow roads restricted our use of large machinery. Then we had about four derelict acres, now we farm around 300 very productive acres with 40 different landlords, which can be complicated when it comes to the paperwork.

"We live in a beautiful part of the island and see it as our duty to maintain the countryside in the best possible way, so recycling is a huge part of what we do. We produce our own crops to feed the animals. We keep the use of sprays and fertiliser to an absolute minimum and encourage farm visits to show people exactly what we do and to explain why we do it. Some of our visitors are farmers, some are restaurateurs and some are members of the public who are interested in farming and in Guernsey."

SLOW-ROASTED BRISKET OF MEADOW COURT FARM BEEF WITH CHASSEUR SAUCE

Serves 6

INGREDIENTS:

1.4kg	Beef brisket
250g	Onions (diced)
300g	Celery (diced)
350g	Carrots (diced)
20g	Fresh Guernsey flat leaf parsley
20g	Fresh Guernsey tarragon stalks
3	Bay leaves
375ml	Red wine
375ml	Beef stock (see page 188)
40g	English mustard
	Sea Salt
	Freshly cracked black peppercorns
50g	Plain flour
30g	Beef dripping or vegetable oil

Chasseur sauce:

50g	Guernsey Dairy butter (diced and chilled)
50g	Guernsey Dairy butter (soft)
75g	Shallots (finely diced)
1 bulb	Garlic (finely chopped)
375ml	Dry white wine
375ml	Beef stock (see page 188)
20g	Fresh Guernsey flat leaf parsley (snipped)
20g	Fresh Guernsey tarragon (snipped)
225g	La Vallees Farm button mushrooms (finely sliced)
25g	Mushroom duxelle (optional – see page 130)
	Yorkshire pudding (see page 198)

METHOD:

Score the brisket of beef with a sharp cook's knife, making equal incisions. Rub the sea salt, freshly cracked peppercorns, garlic and English mustard well into the joint.

In a large baking tray or earthenware dish, sprinkle in half the chopped vegetables. Place on these the joint of beef and add the remaining vegetables.

Cover with the red wine and beef stock and marinate in refrigerator overnight.

The following day, remove the joint from the marinade and

pat dry. Dust with the plain flour and place in a large frying pan with a little oil or beef dripping to seal. Once the joint has browned evenly, return to the marinade and heat gently on the stove. When it reaches simmering point, cover with a well-fitting lid or baking foil and place in a low oven at 160°C, 325°F or Gas 3 for up to 5 hours. When cooked and tender, carefully remove from the braising liquor and serve carved with the chasseur sauce.

To prepare the chasseur sauce, melt the softened butter in a large saucepan, add the finely diced shallots and cook gently for 2-3 minutes without colouring. Add the sliced mushrooms and cook for a further 1-2 minutes.

Pour into a colander to allow the cooking butter to drain off. Return the shallots and mushrooms to the cleaned saucepan and add the dry white wine.

Bring to simmering point and allow to simmer until reduced by half in volume.

Add the beef stock together with a dessertspoon of mushroom duxelle*, if required, and cook gently for a further 10-15 minutes until the sauce has reduced and thickened enough to lightly coat the back of a spoon.

Prior to serving, remove the saucepan from the direct heat and whisk in the remaining iced butter, one piece at a time, together with the snipped fresh Guernsey herbs. This will both lightly thicken and enrich the sauce.

*The optional mushroom duxelle heightens the flavour of the sauce. It can be made in advance and stored for up to two weeks in a sealed refrigerated container.

FILLET OF MEADOW COURT FARM STEAK, BLUE CHEESE BONBONS, MUSHROOM DUXELLE & ROCKET SALAD

Serves 4

INGREDIENTS:

4x225g	Fillet steaks
250g	Fresh Guernsey rocket salad
	Sea Salt
	Freshly ground black pepper
5ml	Balsamic glaze

Mushroom duxelle:

25g	Guernsey Dairy butter
450g	La Vallee's Farm mushrooms
60g	Shallots (finely chopped)
20g	Fresh Guernsey tarragon
25ml	Madeira wine
50ml	Guernsey Dairy whipping cream

Blue cheese bonbons:

60g	Torteval blue cheese
150g	Mashed potato
1	Free range egg yolk
25ml	Guernsey Dairy cream

To coat the bonbons:

150g	Plain flour
1	Free range egg
50ml	Guernsey Dairy milk
100g	Breadcrumbs
	Vegetable oil or sunflower oil (for deep frying)

METHOD:

To prepare the blue cheese bonbons, grate the cheese into a bowl containing the mashed potato, add the egg yolk and whisk the cream into the mix. Shape into mini bonbons and set aside in the refrigerator until required.

When chilled, dip each bonbon into a traditional pané of flour, followed by beaten egg and milk and finally into the breadcrumbs. Repeat this process twice if necessary.

For the Mushroom Duxelle, wash the mushrooms under cold water and pat dry. Place in a food processor and blitz.

In a frying pan, gently sauté the chopped shallots in the butter until they soften and become translucent. Add the blitzed mushrooms and cook gently until the liquid has almost evaporated and the mixture begins to thicken. Add the freshly picked tarragon leaves, Madeira wine and cream. Gently reduce the mixture until it has almost formed a paste. Adjust the seasoning and set aside to keep hot.

For the fillet steaks, heat a heavy frying pan (or two) until very hot and almost smoking.

Remember, too many steaks in one pan will reduce the heat of the frying very quickly and affect the cooking of the steak.

Season both sides of the steaks well with salt and pepper and rub a little olive oil into each side.

Cook the steaks on one side only for 4-5 minutes or until the meat begins to caramelise and show a good brown colour on the underneath – the heat will visibly progress through the steak.

Turn the steaks over and cook for a further 3-6 minutes on the reverse side, depending on preference.

When the steaks are almost cooked, remove from the direct heat and place the frying pans in a warm area to allow the steaks to 'rest'.

Reserve any juices which may come from the steaks.

Deep fry the blue cheese bonbons in hot vegetable or sunflower oil for a couple of minutes until golden. Remove from the hot oil using a slotted spoon and drain on kitchen paper.

Divide the mushroom duxelle onto the chosen serving dishes and place a steak alongside on each plate. Add the blue cheese bonbons and serve together with a side of washed rocket leaves tossed in the reserved beef juices with a little balsamic glaze.

MEADOW COURT FARM BEEF 'N' 'CYNFUL ALE' PIE

Serves 4

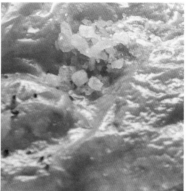

INGREDIENTS:

1 litre	'Cynful Ale' (or your preferred local ale)
1kg	Guernsey beef chuck steak (cut into 2cm dice)
250g	Mushrooms
125g	Belly pork (finely chopped)
2	Onions (peeled & sliced)
300g	Carrots (peeled & sliced)
250g	Baby onions/shallots (peeled)
50g	Plain flour
200ml	Beef stock (see page 188)
1	Clove of garlic (crushed)
1	Bay leaf
6-8	Sprigs of thyme
	Salt
	Freshly crushed black pepper
250-300g	Puff pastry
1	Free range egg (beaten)

METHOD:

Heat the Cynful mild to boiling point in a large saucepan and simmer until reduced to approximately one-third of its original volume.

Heat a large frying pan and fry the diced beef in oil until it is sealed. Sprinkle a little plain flour into the pan and stir. The flour will brown slightly as it cooks with the diced beef and any excess fat.

Meanwhile, cover the bottom of a heavy casserole dish with the onions, followed by the carrots, the beef, baby onions, herbs, belly pork, mushrooms and crushed garlic. Season each layer as you go.

Add the beef stock to the reduced beer and reheat.

Pour the liquid onto the layered casserole dish and cover with a tight-fitting lid.

Place the sealed casserole into a pre-heated oven – 150°C, 300°F, Gas 2 for approximately 2½ hours.

Meanwhile, roll out the puff pastry until approximately 5mm thick and slightly larger in diameter than your casserole dish. Remove the casserole from the oven and using a rolling pin, lift the pastry and place it over the top of the dish. Crimp the overhanging pastry with your fingers and thumb to create a seal. Brush the surface of the pastry with a beaten egg. Pierce the pastry with a sharp knife to allow any steam to release and return to the oven for 30-40 minutes before serving with creamy mashed potatoes, buttered carrots and braised red cabbage. (See page 196).

MEADOW COURT FARM MEATBALLS, GUERNSEY TOMATO & BASIL SAUCE

Serves 4

INGREDIENTS:

Meatballs:

600g	Meadow Court Farm beef mince (or similar from your butcher)
1	Onion (finely diced)
20g	Fresh Guernsey flat leaf parsley
20g	Fresh Guernsey chives
30ml	Guernsey Dairy milk
2	Slices stale bread
30g	Parmesan cheese
1	Free range egg
100g	Plain flour
100ml	Olive oil

Tomato & basil sauce:

1	Onion (finely diced)
1	Clove garlic
1	Orange (zest of)
800g	Ripe tomatoes (chopped)
40g	Fresh Guernsey basil
1/2	Fennel bulb
25g	Tomato paste
20ml	Olive oil
	Pinch of sugar
	Sea salt
	Freshly-ground black peppercorns

METHOD:

Pour the milk into a large bowl together with the stale bread and allow to soak. Mash the mixture together to form a paste. Set aside.

Place the minced beef into a separate large bowl together with the onion and herbs, season well with salt and freshly-ground peppercorns.

Mix the bread and milk mixture together with the minced beef mixture, a beaten egg and grated parmesan cheese. Mix well together.

Before shaping the meatballs, check the seasoning and consistency by frying a small ball in olive oil as a tester. Shape the remaining mixture into 5cm diameter meatballs by rolling in the hand, using a little plain flour to prevent them sticking to your hands. Set aside until required.

In a large non-stick saucepan, heat the olive oil over a moderate heat, add the meatballs and cook until browned evenly, turning them over gently to prevent any breaking. Remove from heat and drain off any excess oil. Set the meatballs to one side on kitchen paper.

Fresh Guernsey tomato & basil sauce:

Heat the olive oil in a large saucepan over a moderate heat. Fry the onion and shredded fennel for approximately 5 minutes until soft and translucent. Add the chopped ripe tomatoes together with chopped garlic, tomato purée, a pinch of sugar and finely-grated zest of one orange.

Bring to simmering point and reduce the heat. Cook gently for 30 minutes. Blitz with a blender and place in a pan with the meatballs. Simmer for a further 20-25 minutes before adding shredded, freshly-picked basil leaves. Check seasoning and serve.

Tony Leck's Pavilion on a Plate

Tony Leck's Pavilion on a Plate

GUERNSEY DAIRY

Guernsey Dairy products have a worldwide reputation for quality. Our butter in particular is very popular with islanders and lends itself to cooking uses and for complementing freshly baked breads or the locally-produced Gâche (a type of fruit loaf – see recipe page 182).

What makes it special is the not generally-appreciated fact that the seasons, along with the cow's diet, cause slight colour variations in the milk, which go some way to enhancing the natural appeal of both the cream and butter.

We have some 2,000 cattle on the island. It is believed that they were originally brought here by monks banished from Mont St Michel across the water in France and then bred with stronger, high milk-producing breeds. The result is our beautiful Golden Guernsey.

None of our milk ever goes to waste. Our dairy is owned by the states of Guernsey and it is required by law to buy all the milk produced by the island farmers, all of them independent.

I use Guernsey Dairy products every day for almost every recipe. They are fresh, readily available and above all home-grown – what more could you ask?

"Being the only dairy on the island has its challenges as well as its rewards," said Andrew Tabel, general manager, who was born and bred on Guernsey.

"It's been that way since the early 1900s. The way it is farmed has changed considerably. In the 1930s there were about 400 farmers with six or seven cows each. Today we have 18 dairy farmers with herds in the hundreds. With its central island location in the parish of St. Andrews, each farm is within three miles proximity of the Dairy – food miles are certainly not an issue here!"

Approximately 8.1 million litres of milk is processed by the dairy every year. Of that, 6.6 million litres is put into cartons and sold on the island. The rest is used by the dairy to make 300,000kg of butter and 57 tonnes of award-winning cheese, 116,000 litres of cream and 110,000 litres of dairy ice cream.

The Dairy funds its own activities and reinvests any operating surplus back into the business. "And we listen to our customers," said Andrew. "We keep up with changing tastes, using no colouring or additives. Everything is as natural as can be. We still have doorstep deliveries and the cartons we use are recycled on the island."

Although all the milk and cream produced by the Dairy is bought locally, Golden Guernsey butter is exported to the UK and there are Guernsey cows to be found on every continent.

CRÈME CARAMEL

Serves 4-5

INGREDIENTS:

Caramel:

100g   Granulated sugar

Custard:

450ml   Guernsey Dairy milk

75g   Caster sugar

4   Free range eggs

1   Vanilla pod

METHOD:

N.B. This recipe involves boiling sugar which reaches high temperatures.

Work carefully; always have either a saucepan or jug of cold water nearby or access to cold water in case of any spillage or accident.

To prepare the caramel, place the granulated sugar in a very clean saucepan with 2 teaspoons of water, stir and dissolve over a gentle heat. Once dissolved, increase the heat and boil rapidly until a light caramel colour. Remove the saucepan from the heat and allow to deepen slightly in colour. The colour of the caramel has a huge effect on the finished flavour of this dish, too dark and the dish will be bitter, too blonde and the dessert will be sickly sweet! Aim for a deep brown result. If the caramel is looking like it is continuing to deepen in colour, place the base of the saucepan into a larger bowl of cold water which will reduce the heat of the saucepan and prevent further cooking.

Pour the caramel into chosen ramekin moulds.

Prepare the custard by heating the milk in a saucepan together with the seeds scraped from one vanilla pod.

Meanwhile whisk together the eggs and sugar. Once the milk has reached scalding point, pour over the egg and sugar mix and whisk together. Pour through a fine sieve. Place the ramekins in a deep roasting or baking tray half filled with water. Pour the custard into the ramekins and place in a pre-heated oven at 150°C, 300°F, Gas 2 for approximately 35 minutes or until just set.

Remove from the oven and tray and leave to cool. Serve chilled by upturning the mould and lightly running a knife around the edge of the ramekin dish. Serve with Guernsey Dairy whipping cream and some seasonal fresh fruits of your preference.

LEMON CRÈME BRÛLÉE

Serves 4

INGREDIENTS:

600ml	Guernsey whipping cream
	Vanilla pod (split lengthways)
2	Lemons (zest of)
2	Free range eggs
4	Free range egg yolks
75g	Caster sugar
75g	Soft brown Demerara sugar

METHOD:

Pre-heat oven to 140°C, 275°F, Gas 1.

Whisk together the eggs, yolks and sugar until light, white and fluffy in appearance.

Meanwhile bring the cream to scalding point with the vanilla pod and lemon zest and allow to infuse in the cream for approximately 10 minutes before re-heating to boiling point. Pour this cream onto the egg mixture and whisk together. Pour through a sieve and into individual ramekin dishes.

Place the ramekin dishes onto a deep tray and pour around them hot water almost as deep as the dishes, and place in a pre-heated oven.

Bake for approximately 30 minutes or until set. Remove from the oven and allow to cool.

Prior to serving sprinkle the top of each brûlée carefully with a little of the Demerara sugar and place under a hot grill to caramelize the sugar.

Allow to cool before serving. Serve with lemon and vanilla shortbread.

LEMON & VANILLA SHORTBREAD

Makes 10-12 pieces

INGREDIENTS:

200g	Plain flour
100g	Light Muscovado sugar
100g	Unsalted Guernsey butter
1	Vanilla pod (split lengthways and seeds scraped out)
3	Lemons (zest)
	Caster sugar for dredging

METHOD:

Pre-heat the oven to 180°C, 350°F, Gas 4.

Beat together the sugar, butter, vanilla pod seeds and zest of lemons until light and fluffy.

Sieve the flour well and rub into this the creamed butter until the mixture resembles breadcrumbs.

Now knead the pastry very gently so as not to over work the mix.

Roll out onto a lightly floured baking tray to approx. ½cm thickness and shape of your choice. Prick the shortbread evenly with a fork to prevent any uneven rising whilst baking. Bake for 20-25 minutes until pale golden in colour.

Remove from the oven and dredge with caster sugar while still hot and return to the oven for a further 5 minutes at a reduced temperature of 160°C, 325°F, Gas 3.

Remove from the oven and cut into desired shapes or portions whilst the shortbread is still hot.

RHUBARB PANNACOTTA WITH FRIED CUSTARD

Serves 4-6

INGREDIENTS:

100ml	Rhubarb (puréed)
150ml	Guernsey whipping cream
150ml	Guernsey milk
50g	Caster sugar
1	Vanilla pod (split lengthways)
125g	Soft Guernsey goats' cheese
25g	Poached rhubarb
1½	Gelatine leaves

Fried custard:

600ml	Guernsey milk
90g	Caster sugar
1	Vanilla pod (split lengthways)
25g	Cornflour
2	Free range eggs
75g	Ground almonds
	Fresh strawberries

METHOD:

Place the leaf gelatine in a small bowl with half of the cold rhubarb purée. Leave to soften for several minutes.

To poach the rhubarb, firstly peel the stalks with a vegetable peeler. Cut into battons and lightly poach in a little stock syrup. Allow to cool and remove from syrup. (See stock syrup recipe on page 208).

Bring the milk and cream to boiling point with the sugar and vanilla pod.

Remove from the heat, discard the vanilla pod and pour the hot liquid onto the rhubarb purée with the added gelatine and stir until the gelatine has dissolved.

Whisk the soft goats' cheese into the hot cream mixture and pour onto the remaining rhubarb purée before pouring through a fine sieve.

Allow to cool before adding the prepared and poached diced rhubarb and spooning the cooled mixture into desired moulds.

Chill for at least 2 hours.

Turn out from the moulds by briefly immersing the moulds in hot water.

For the fried custard:

Drop the vanilla pod into the milk and bring to the boil.

Whilst heating the milk, whisk together the eggs, cornflour and sugar.

Add the hot milk and stir thoroughly before returning to a clean saucepan.

Place over a low heat and allow to 'cook out' gently whilst continually stirring with a wooden spoon until the custard thickens almost to a paste.

Remove from the heat and pass through a fine sieve using a spatula if necessary.

Place the cooked custard on a flat tray and spread to a thickness of approximately 1cm. Cover with clingfilm and allow to cool.

Once the paste has set and chilled, cut into small chunks.

Dip each shape into sieved flour, followed by beaten egg mixture and finally roll in ground almonds.

Deep fry in vegetable oil prior to serving with rhubarb pannacotta and fresh strawberries.

MILK A PUNCH

The first day in May and also the first Sunday in the month were traditionally marked by customs and celebrations in the Channel Islands, but now only Alderney continues the once Channel Island-wide custom of 'Milk a Punch Sunday' by providing free milk punch to customers in the islands bars and clubs.

INGREDIENTS:

8	Free range eggs
180g	Caster sugar
600ml	Alderney dairy milk
300ml	Dark rum
	Freshly ground nutmeg to taste
	Freshly ground cinnamon to taste

METHOD:

Whisk the free range eggs until foamy and light in texture, add the dark rum and sugar and place into a double boiler over a hot water bath. Constantly whisk the mixture until it holds its trail when the whisk is removed.

Add the freshly ground spices to the milk and bring to boiling point in a large saucepan. Pour the scalded milk onto the whisked egg mixture and serve.

MILK A PUNCH PANNACOTTA

Serves 4

INGREDIENTS:

350ml	Guernsey Dairy whipping cream
60ml	Dark rum
50g	Caster sugar
1	Vanilla pod
125g	Mascarpone cheese
2	Gelatine leaves
½ tsp	Freshly ground nutmeg
¼ tsp	Freshly ground cinnamon

METHOD:

Place the leaf gelatine into a small bowl with the dark rum, leave to soften for several minutes.

Bring to boiling point the cream, sugar and freshly ground spices.

Remove from heat and scrape the seeds from the vanilla pod.

Place the dark rum and gelatine over the hot saucepan until the gelatine has dissolved, do not boil this gelatine mixture. Pour into the hot cream.

Whisk the Mascarpone into the hot cream mixture and pour through a fine sieve.

Allow cooling before pouring into ramekins.

Refrigerate for 3 hours until set or overnight prior to serving.

CHILLED STRAWBERRY RICE PUDDING WITH STRAWBERRY ICE CREAM

Ice cream maker required. Serves 8

INGREDIENTS:

Rice pudding:

60g	Short grain rice
600ml	Guernsey milk
25g	Caster sugar
15g	Unsalted Guernsey butter
150ml	Guernsey whipping cream
1	Leaf of gelatine
1	Vanilla pod (split lengthways)

Strawberry sauce

500g	Fresh strawberries (hulled and washed)
75g	Icing sugar
	Juice of half a lemon

Strawberry jelly

150ml	Strawberry sauce
1½	Leaves of gelatine
100ml	Stock syrup

Strawberry ice cream

250ml	Guernsey Dairy whipping cream
150g	Caster sugar
250ml	Strawberries (puréed)
	Garden mint sprigs

METHOD:

For the rice pudding:

Wash the rice in cold running water and drain through a fine sieve. Place in a saucepan with the butter and heat gently whilst stirring.

Heat the milk in a separate saucepan and pour onto the rice when boiling. Add a split vanilla pod before lowering the heat and cooking gently for 20-25 minutes, stirring occasionally then add the caster sugar.

Soak the gelatine in a little cold water to soften; once softened, squeeze out any excess water and stir into the rice once it is cooked to your liking. Ensure the rice does not boil or cook any further after the gelatine has been added.

Set aside to cool. Remove the vanilla pod, whip the cream to soft peak stage and fold into the rice mixture.

Pour into moulds and place in the fridge for approximately 1 hour to set.

Remember not to fill the moulds right to the top as you need to allow room for a layer of strawberry jelly on the top.

Strawberry sauce

Blitz the washed and hulled strawberries in a liquidiser, together with the icing sugar. Add a little lemon juice (which will help to bring out the flavour).

Pour through a fine sieve and set aside ready to serve with the chilled pudding.

Strawberry jelly

Soak the leaves of gelatine in a little cold water to soften, squeeze dry.

Bring the stock syrup to the boil, remove from heat and add the gelatine leaves.

Add the strawberry sauce and cool. Once cool and almost at setting point, pour gently over the chilled rice pudding mixture and chill for a further 2 hours or more.

Strawberry ice cream

Bring the cream and caster sugar to the boil. Scald and simmer for 30 seconds. Remove from heat.

Add the washed and hulled strawberries. Blitz in a liquidiser. Allow to cool before churning in an ice cream maker.

To serve

Remove the puddings from their moulds and place some hulled strawberries on the top. Pour over the reserved strawberry sauce and serve immediately with the freshly made strawberry ice cream. Garnish with freshly picked sprigs of garden mint.

Tony Leck's Pavilion on a Plate

STRAWBERRY SHORTCAKE

Serves 6

INGREDIENTS:

Shortcake:

240g	Unsalted Guernsey butter
110g	Icing sugar
240g	Plain flour (sieved)
40g	Rice flour

Strawberries:

500g	Strawberries
50g	Icing sugar
5ml	Balsamic vinegar
	Freshly milled black peppercorns
100ml	Strawberry coulis (see page 204)
284ml	Guernsey Dairy extra thick cream
1	Vanilla pod (split)
	Sprigs of freshly picked mint

METHOD:

Beat together the unsalted butter and sugar until pale in colour, light and creamy in texture.

Sieve into this mixture the flour and rice flour. Cover the paste with clingfilm and set aside to rest the paste for 30 minutes. (The paste can also be rolled into a large sausage shape at this stage, wrapped in film and stored in the freezer for another day. Once removed from the freezer and allowed to thaw you can simply slice rounds off ready to bake.)

Roll the shortcake paste out onto a work top, lightly dusted with flour and cut out discs with a 10cm cutter.

Place these shortcakes on a baking sheet and bake at 140°C, 275°F or Gas 1 for 30-35 minutes until light golden in colour.

Remove from baking tray and once cool set aside in a sealed container until ready to assemble.

Prepare the strawberries by washing and hulling them.

Pat the fruit dry very gently with kitchen paper and place on a tray. Dust them with the icing sugar and leave to macerate for half an hour or more at room temperature before assembling the dessert for serving.

To serve the shortcake, mix the seeds of the vanilla pod together with the extra thick Guernsey cream. Assemble each shortcake with a sandwich style filling of macerated strawberries and cream. Season with a splash of balsamic vinegar and freshly ground peppercorns.

Dust each top layer of shortcake with icing sugar.

Pour onto the plates a little strawberry coulis and add a sprig of freshly picked mint.

PEPPERED STRAWBERRIES WITH GUERNSEY BUTTER BISCUITS AND BASIL ICE CREAM

Serves 4

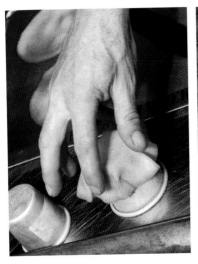

INGREDIENTS:

450g	Fresh Guernsey strawberries
250ml	Basil ice cream (see page 212)
10g	Icing sugar
	Vanilla pod (split lengthways)
	Freshly ground black pepper

Guernsey butter biscuits:

2	Free range egg whites
40g	Plain flour (sieved)
50g	Icing sugar (sieved)
60g	Unsalted Guernsey butter
100ml	Strawberry sauce or strawberry coulis (see page 204)

METHOD:

Hull the strawberries and sprinkle with the icing sugar and scraped seeds from the vanilla pod. Leave to macerate in the refrigerator.

Guernsey butter biscuits:

Whisk together the egg whites with the icing sugar, add the flour and mix to a paste. Melt the butter and add to the paste to make a batter.

Set aside this batter in the refrigerator to allow to rest for 30 minutes.

Then spread the batter thinly onto lightly greased baking sheets or onto baking mats in round shapes.

Bake at 165°C, 330°F or Gas 3-4 for 3-4 minutes until a light golden colour. Whilst still hot, remove from the trays and mould over an upturned cup or a ramekin dish to create a basket shape. The paste will set crisp immediately on cooling.

Scoop the basil ice cream and place with the strawberries in each basket, pour around some strawberry sauce before serving immediately with freshly ground black peppercorns from the mill.

APPLE & CALVADOS BABA WITH NUTMEG ICE CREAM

Serves 6

INGREDIENTS:

Dough:

120g	Strong flour
90g	Eggs (lightly beaten & sieved)
10g	Yeast
15g	Water
60g	Guernsey Dairy butter (unsalted & melted)
60g	Chopped apple
15g	Caster sugar

Syrup:

120g	Caster sugar
150ml	Water
80ml	Calvados
Pinch	Cinnamon
½	Orange

Glaze:

125ml	Apricot Jam

METHOD:

Prepare a dough by adding the yeast and sugar to the warm water. Mix this with the sieved strong flour and the lightly beaten and sieved eggs. This dough should be mixed well until smooth and elastic (ideally at a temperature of approximately 27°C, 80°F).

Allow the dough to rest for about 30 minutes in a warm place. Keep it covered to prevent a skin or crust forming.

When the dough has proved, gradually beat in the melted butter to create a batter-style dough, then add the chopped apple.

Grease individual dariole moulds and dust each with a little flour. Tap out any excess flour.

Divide the batter/dough equally filling the dariole dishes approximately one-third full.

Allow to prove fully before baking at 230°C, 450°F, Gas 8 for 20-25 minutes.

Remove from moulds while still warm and set aside on a cooling rack.

Heat all the ingredients for the syrup together and boil for 1-2 minutes in a large saucepan. Allow the flavours to infuse for several minutes before pouring through a sieve.

When the Babas cool, saturate each one by dipping into the warmed syrup using a slotted kitchen spoon or similar. Allow them to drain naturally. Any excess or surplus syrup can be reheated and used in other dishes.

Prepare an apricot glaze by boiling the apricot jam together with 50ml water for 2 minutes. Pour through a sieve and glaze each Baba using a pastry brush.

Serve with homemade nutmeg ice cream. (See page 211)

BAKED CUSTARD TART WITH NUTMEG

Serves 6

INGREDIENTS:

250g	Sweet shortcrust pastry (see page 206)
2	Free range eggs
4	Free range egg yolks
80g	Caster sugar
150ml	Guernsey Dairy whipping cream
300ml	Guernsey Dairy full cream milk
1	Vanilla pod (split)
5ml	Rosewater essence
10g	Freshly grated nutmeg

METHOD:

Blind bake an 18cm diameter tart case using sweet paste. Once baked to a golden colour, paint the inside of the pastry case with a beaten egg and return to the oven for a couple of minutes. This will create a seal and ensure the filling won't leak from the tart and the base stays crisp. Set aside.

In a heavy-based saucepan, heat the Guernsey Dairy milk and cream to boiling point together with the split vanilla pod.

Whisk the eggs, egg yolks and sugar together for a couple of minutes.

Pour onto this the hot milk and cream and stir well. Strain through a fine sieve into a large pouring jug, add the rosewater essence and whisk in.

Carefully pour this liquid into the pre-baked pastry case and sprinkle the freshly grated nutmeg over the top. Bake at 160°C, 325°F or Gas 3 for 30 minutes or until the filling is slightly wobbly but almost set.

When cooked, remove from the oven and leave to cool before serving. This dish can be served chilled.

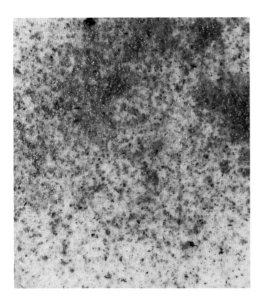

LEMON TART

Serves 6-8
1 x 27cm tart ring

INGREDIENTS:

Pastry:

125g	Unsalted Guernsey butter
110g	Icing sugar
250g	Plain flour (sieved)
40g	Ground almonds
2	Free range eggs
1	Lemon (zest)
1	Vanilla pod (seeds)
	Extra flour for dusting
1	Egg yolk for pastry case.

Filling:

284ml	Guernsey Dairy whipping cream
4	Free range eggs
2	Free range egg yolks
200g	Caster sugar
2	Lemons (zest)
3	Lemons (juice)
1	Vanilla pod (seeds)

METHOD:

To make the pastry, lightly beat the eggs and set aside. Place the diced unsalted butter, icing sugar and sieved plain flour in a cold mixing bowl, add the finely grated zest of one lemon and the seeds scraped from a vanilla pod. Mix all these ingredients together lightly with your hands until a crumb or sand texture is achieved. Add to this the beaten egg. Be careful not to add all at once as eggs can vary slightly in size and not all may be required. Cover pastry with clingfilm and set aside in the refrigerator for 30 minutes.

Lightly dust your table top with flour and roll out the pastry as thin as is possible, (approximately 2-3mm thick). Line a pre-greased or non-stick tart ring with the pastry and allow the excess to overhang the sides. Set the pastry ring aside to rest in the refrigerator for 30 minutes.

Pre–heat the oven to 180°C, 350°F or Gas 5.

Cover the inside of the tart with a layer of clingfilm or baking parchment paper and fill with either baking beans or dried rice. Bake the tart 'blind' for 20-25 minutes until golden in colour and the base is evenly cooked.

Remove the rice/beans and paper or clingfilm. Using a pastry brush, paint the inside of the tart with the extra egg yolk and return the pastry case to the oven for 2 minutes to create a seal and prevent any filling from leaking whilst helping the finished dish retain a crisp base.

Remove from the oven and, using a sharp knife, remove any excess pastry.

For the filling:

To prepare the filling, whisk together the eggs, egg yolks, sugar and juice of three lemons. In a saucepan bring the cream to scalding point together with the seeds of a vanilla pod and zest of two lemons, pour onto the whisked mixture and mix together.

Pour filling into the tart ring and place in an oven at a reduced temperature of 125-130°C, 240-250°F or Gas 1 for 30-40 minutes depending on the depth of the tart ring.

Remove from oven and allow to cool.

Prior to serving, dust the tart with a little icing sugar and place under a hot grill for a few seconds to create a caramelized crisp texture on the top.

Serve with freshly picked raspberries and extra thick Guernsey Dairy cream.

RASPBERRY ARCTIC ROLL WITH SUMMER BERRIES

An ice cream maker is needed for this recipe

INGREDIENTS:

Ice cream

500ml	Guernsey Dairy whipping cream
300g	Caster sugar
500ml	Raspberry purée
250g	Fresh raspberries
100ml	Raspberry jam
250g	Summer berries

Sponge

4	Free range eggs
80g	Caster sugar
65g	Plain flour (sieved)
1	Lime (zest)
20g	Caster sugar (for dusting)

METHOD:

For the ice cream:

Purée the fresh raspberries and pass through a fine sieve.

In a saucepan bring the cream and sugar to scalding point and remove from the heat. Allow to cool. When chilled, add the puréed raspberries and proceed to churn in an ice cream machine.

Once ready, spread several layers of cling film onto a clean chilled work bench. Spoon half the ice cream onto this and stud with some fresh raspberries. Roll the cling film around the ice cream to create a sausage or log shape approximately 5cm in diameter and 30cm long. Repeat this process to create two logs. Place these logs into the freezer overnight to set.

For the sponge:

Pre-heat the oven to 190°C, 375°F or Gas 5 and line a flat baking sheet with parchment paper. Place the 80g caster sugar on a separate piece of parchment paper and place in the oven for 2-3 minutes to warm through. Meanwhile whisk the eggs until white light and fluffy. Remove the sugar from the oven and gradually add to the eggs, continue whisking until thick and doubled in volume. Fold in the sieved flour lightly together with the finely grated lime zest.

Spread the sponge mixture approximately 0.5 cm thick onto the tray with a palette knife, bake for 4-5 minutes. Once cooked, remove from the oven immediately and sprinkle the sponge with the remaining caster sugar. Keep the parchment paper on the sponge and roll the cake like a Swiss Roll.

Once cool, unroll and spread a thin layer of raspberry jam over the inside of the sponge. Remove the prepared ice cream from the freezer and place onto the sponge. Re-roll into sausage shape again, using cling film and return to the freezer until required.

To serve, slice the Arctic Roll into portions and serve with extra thick Guernsey Dairy cream and a selection of fresh seasonal summer berries.

FLOATING ISLANDS

Serves 6

INGREDIENTS:

Meringue:

225g	Free range egg whites (from approx. seven medium eggs)
275g	Caster sugar

Vanilla custard:

1 litre	Guernsey Dairy milk
200g	Caster sugar
8	Free range egg yolks
1	Vanilla Pod (halved lengthways with the seeds scraped out)

Decoration:

100g	Caster sugar

METHOD:

Whisk the egg whites in a bowl with one-third of the sugar until soft peaks are formed. Gradually add the remaining sugar, whisking constantly until all is incorporated and the mixture forms stiff peaks.

Note: The bowl and any utensils should be clean and free from any traces of grease or water as this will prevent the egg whites from forming the meringue.

Once the meringue is stiff, spoon into individual pastry rings and smooth the top with a palette knife to give them all a regular shape.

Bring the milk to scalding point together with the split vanilla pod. Remove from direct heat and gently add the pastry rings to poach the meringues. Turn the meringues over occasionally until they are evenly cooked, i.e. firm in consistency and dry in appearance. Remove from the poaching liquor and set aside to cool. Then transfer to the refrigerator where they will retain their shape better and will be easier to release from the pastry rings as they will contract very slightly.

Prepare the custard by whisking together the egg yolks and caster sugar until white in colour and light in texture. Combine with the poaching liquor and return to a gentle heat. Scrape the seeds from the vanilla pod and add to the pan. Stir constantly until the custard begins to thicken slightly and coats the back of a spoon whilst stirring.

Pass the custard through a fine sieve and allow to cool.

To serve:

Pour the chilled custard into the desired bowls or glasses and gently place a poached meringue into each.

In a non-stick saucepan, melt 100g of caster sugar over a moderate heat, stirring constantly to ensure even colouring. Once a golden caramel colour, remove from heat source and, using a fork or a spoon dipped into the hot caramel, trail the spoon or fork over the dessert to form a caramel decoration.

This recipe involves melting sugar which reaches high temperatures.

Work carefully; always have either a saucepan or jug of cold water nearby or access to cold water in case of any spillage or accident.

Floating Islands is a favourite dessert, regularly featured on restaurant menus on both sides of the Channel.

Also known as Ile flottante, Ouefs á la Neige or Snow Eggs, I believe it is one of the simplest dishes to make using only eggs, milk and sugar; each ingredient has more than one use in the preparation which makes this a very good recipe to test 'housekeeping' skills!

ROCQUETTE CIDER CHEESECAKE

Serves 8-10 (1 x 27cm ring)

INGREDIENTS:

Biscuit base:

150g	Honey & oatmeal biscuits (see page 202)
75g	Unsalted Guernsey Dairy butter

Rocquette cider jelly:

200ml	Rocquette cider
120g	Caster sugar
50ml	Still spring water
2	Gelatine leaves
1	Lemon (juice)

Cheesecake filling:

250ml	Rocquette cider
30g	Caster sugar
250g	Soft cream cheese
484ml	Guernsey Dairy whipping cream
5	Leaves of gelatine
1	Apple (peeled, cored and finley-diced)

METHOD:

Crush the oatcakes and mix together with melted unsalted butter. Place this into the base of a pastry ring, pat down and set aside.

For the Rocquette cider jelly:

Place the leaf gelatine in a small bowl with the water. Leave to soften for several minutes.

Bring the Rocquette cider, lemon juice and sugar to boiling point.

Remove from heat and add the gelatine and water.

Pour through a fine sieve and set aside at room temperature for later use.

For the cheesecake filling:

Soak the gelatine in a little water until soft and pliable.

In a saucepan, add the cider, caster sugar and diced apple and bring to a gentle heat. Simmer for 2-3 minutes until slightly reduced in volume.

Remove from heat and add the softenend gelatine leaves stirring until completely dissolved. In a bowl combine this mixture with the soft cream cheese and whisk together until smooth and cool.

In a separate bowl, whip the cream until soft peaks are formed. Gently fold this into the cream cheese mixture.

Spoon over the crushed biscuit base and spread the surface with a palette knife to create a flat smooth surface, approximately 1cm below the lip of the pastry ring.

Set aside in the fridge until set.

Once set, pour over the Rocquette cider jelly and return to the fridge until that layer has also set.

To serve, remove from the pastry ring and slice. Serve with blackberries and sloe gin custard. (See page 209).

Tony Leck's Pavilion on a Plate

TRADITIONAL GUERNSEY GÂCHE MELÉE
WITH MARMALADE ICE CREAM

INGREDIENTS:

350g	Plain flour
150g	Wholemeal flour
600g	Cooking apples (peeled, cored & diced)
250g	Guernsey Dairy unsalted butter or beef suet
250g	Demerara sugar
3-4	Free range eggs
1 tsp	Ground cinnamon
1	Nutmeg (grated)
125ml	Guernsey Dairy milk (optional)
1	Lemon (zest)

METHOD:

Peel, core and dice the apple finely and scatter into a large earthenware or ovenproof dish. Sprinkle with the grated spices and zest of lemon.

Mix the plain and wholemeal flour together and grate into this the cold butter or beef suet depending on your preference.

Scatter over the apples and leave for 2-3 hours to allow the flour to absorb the juice from the apples.

Whisk together the demerara sugar and eggs until light in texture. Fold this mixture into the flour and apple mixture and stir until all is combined.

Add a little milk if the mixture seems too stiff or dry.

Place mixture into a buttered cake tin and bake at 170°C, 325°F, Gas 3 for 60-70 minutes until golden brown. Serve with Guernsey Dairy cream, custard or marmalade ice cream (below).

Guernsey Gâche is pronounced 'GOSH'
Gâche is the Norman French word for cake.

MARMALADE ICE CREAM

INGREDIENTS:

500ml	Guernsey milk
55g	Caster sugar
6	Free range eggs
100ml	Guernsey whipping cream
120g	Orange marmalade

METHOD:

Prepare as for basic vanilla ice cream (see page 213). Use thick cut marmalade for more texture and superior flavour.

Marmalade surely is a great comfort food. You can't beat it for breakfast, spread over crisp warm toast with lashings of butter. But marmalade also deserves the opportunity to star as part of a comforting dessert.

Guernsey's capital town, St Peter Port, was the world's largest overseas trader of the preserve during the 19th Century, which inspired me to 'spread' some marmalade to our dessert menu!

In 1857 James Kellar & Son of Dundee, Scotland, celebrated pioneers of marmalade manufacturing, set up a branch in Guernsey. Its purpose was to evade costly duties on sugar. Unfortunately, after 1879 when Britain itself permitted the free importing of sugar, the business transferred to a larger new factory at Silver Town on the Thames.

WARM GÂCHE MELÉE CHEESECAKE

A baked cheesecake served just warm with hot custard and/or with clove ice cream! Apples and cheese complement each other particularly well; in my native North of England there is a saying: "Apple pie without cheese is like a kiss without a squeeze." I have adapted a warm cheesecake recipe, combining it with a traditional local pudding recipe of Gâche Melée.

INGREDIENTS:

250g	Sweet shortcrust pastry (see page 206)
350g	Soft Guernsey goats' cheese
150g	Caster sugar
8 tbsp	Guernsey double cream
2	Medium apples (peeled, cored and diced)
3	Free range eggs
2	Free range egg yolks
30g	Corn flour
60g	Sultanas
	Pinch of ground cinnamon and nutmeg

METHOD:

Line a 27cm diameter flan ring with sweet shortcrust pastry.

Pre-heat the oven to 180°C, 350°F, Gas 4 and bake the pastry blind until just set.

Mix together the goats' cheese and double cream. Add the sugar and ground spices then whisk together well.

Peel, core and chop the apples and add to the cream and cheese mixture.

Separate the eggs and whisk the five egg yolks briskly with the corn flour. Add this gradually to the cream and cheese mixture. Fold in the sultanas.

In a clean bowl, whisk the egg whites stiffly, adding the remaining caster sugar as the egg whites peak. Fold this into the mixture.

Spread the wet mix into the pre-baked pastry case and bake for 10 minutes at 180°C, 350°F, Gas 4.

Reduce heat to 150°C, 300°F, Gas 2 and bake for a further 35-40 minutes.

Remove from the oven and leave to cool before serving.

Serve with hot sultana custard (see page 213) or clove ice cream (see page 211), or if you prefer, both!

GUERNSEY GÂCHE 'N' BUTTER PUDDING WITH ROCQUETTE CIDER CUSTARD

Serves 6

INGREDIENTS:

Pudding:

1	Loaf of Guernsey gâche (See page 182)
500ml	Guernsey Dairy whipping cream
4	Free range egg yolks
50g	Sugar
50g	Guernsey Dairy unsalted butter
1	Pinch freshly grated nutmeg
1	Orange (zest)
30g	Soft brown sugar

Cider Custard:

125ml	Guernsey Dairy whipping cream
3	Free range egg yolks
50g	Caster sugar
125ml	Rocquette cider
1	Vanilla pod (split lengthways)

METHOD:

To prepare the pudding, cut the gâche into thin slices and place in a buttered ovenproof dish, butter each slice individually. Heat the cream in a saucepan with the orange zest to boiling point. Beat together the egg yolks and sugar.

Mix with the heated cream and pour over the buttered gâche. Sprinkle the top with the soft brown sugar and place in an oven pre-heated to 180°C, 350°F, Gas 4 for approximately 45 minutes.

For the custard, whisk together the sugar and egg yolks. Meanwhile, bring the cream and cider to scalding point together with the vanilla pod. Pour onto the egg mixture and return to a gentle heat, stirring constantly to avoid the mixture overheating and curdling the eggs. This sauce will thicken slightly as the egg yolks cook.

Pour through a sieve and set aside ready to serve with the baked pudding.

POACHED GARDEN PEARS
WITH HEDGEROW BRAMBLES

Serves 6

INGREDIENTS:

6	Firm pears
500ml	Rocquette cider
2	Whole cloves
2	Vanilla pods (split lengthways)
4 tbsp	Caster sugar
3-4	Whole black peppercorns (cracked)
1	Small piece of cinnamon stick
	Thick Guernsey cream
	Blackberries or brambles freshly picked from hedgerows.

METHOD:

Prepare poaching liquor by adding the sugar and Rocquette cider together in a large heavy based saucepan with the spices. Bring this syrup to simmering point.

Peel the pears and remove the core with a Parisienne scoop or a melon baller, slice a little off the base of each pear so they can stand upright once poached. Add the pears to the simmering syrup. Cover with a layer of greaseproof paper, poach gently for approximately 30-35 minutes until the pears are soft and tender, yet still holding their shape.

Remove pears from the syrup and allow to cool.

Continue simmering the poaching liquor in the pan until it has reduced to one third of the original volume and thickened slightly. Pour this over the poached pears and allow to cool.

Serve simply with thick Guernsey cream and blackberries or brambleberries picked from wild hedgerows.

If the blackberries or brambles are a little acidic, pour a little of the warm syrup over them and allow to infuse in a separate bowl.

FIG & ALMOND TART WITH GUERNSEY HONEY & LAVENDER CREAM

Serves 6

INGREDIENTS:

Sweet shortcrust pastry:

Make using approximately one-third of the quantity for sweet shortcrust pastry recipe (see page 206).

Almond sponge:

125g	Guernsey Dairy unsalted butter
125g	Caster sugar
2	Free range eggs
125g	Ground almonds
30g	Plain flour (sieved)
15ml	Almond liqueur
6	Ripe figs
60ml	Guernsey honey
284ml	Guernsey Dairy whipping cream (whipped to soft peaks)
	Sprigs of fresh lavender

METHOD:

Prepare a sweet shortcrust pastry as per recipe. Divide into six even-sized balls and roll each one out into a circular shape on a lightly-floured work surface. Carefully line six 12cm diameter tartlet tins with the pastry. Using a fork, prick the base of each tart to prevent the pastry rising whilst cooking and set aside in the refrigerator to rest for 30 minutes.

To prepare the almond sponge, whisk together the unsalted butter and the sugar until light in texture and white in colour. Gradually whisk into this the two beaten eggs until all is incorporated. Add the liqueur and whisk again. Lightly mix into this the flour and ground almonds. Divide the sponge mix between the tartlet tins, trim off any excess overhanging pastry using a cook's knife.

Place a ripe fig in the centre of each tart and score a cross shape in the top of each one.

Bake at 160°C, 325°F, Gas 3 for 35-40 minutes.

Warm the Guernsey honey carefully with freshly picked lavender, allowing the flavours to infuse. Pour the honey through a sieve and cool before folding into the whipped cream.

Remove the tarts from the oven. Let them cool briefly before serving with the scented Guernsey Cream.

DARK CHOCOLATE TART

Serves 6

For best results, use a superior quality chocolate couverture, one with a minimum of 70% cocoa content. Valrhona is my preferred choice.

INGREDIENTS:

250g	Sweet shortcrust pastry (see page 206)
250g	Dark chocolate (70% cocoa solids)
2	Free range eggs
150ml	Guernsey Dairy whipping cream
100ml	Guernsey Dairy full cream milk

METHOD:

Blind bake an 18cm diameter tart case using sweet pastry. Once baked to a golden colour, paint the inside of the pastry case with a beaten egg and return to the oven for a couple of minutes. This will create a seal and ensure the filling does not leak from the tart. It will also keep the base crisp.

Pre-heat the oven to 180°C, 350°F, Gas 4.

Using a large cook's knife, chop the dark chocolate into small pieces – this will allow it to melt evenly and quickly. Place in a dry bowl over a pan of hot but not boiling water. In a separate saucepan, heat together the cream and the milk until they reach boiling point.

Whisk the eggs lightly and combine with them the hot cream and milk mixture.

Pour the mixture through a sieve onto the liquid chocolate and mix together.

Pour the mixture into the pre-baked tart case and return to the hot oven.

Turn off the oven immediately and leave the chocolate tart there to cool overnight.

Remove and slice into portions. Serve at room temperature with fresh raspberries when in season or raspberry ice cream.

DARK CHOCOLATE & ORANGE MOUSSE

Serves 4 – Note this recipe contains raw eggs.

INGREDIENTS:

200g	Dark chocolate couverture (70% cocoa solids)
2	Free range eggs
300ml	Guernsey Dairy whipping cream
50ml	Cointreau

METHOD:

Using a large cook's knife, chop the dark chocolate couverture into small pieces. Place in a dry bowl.

Heat the cream in a large saucepan until scalding point, pour over the chopped chocolate. Place this mixture into a liquidiser, adding the eggs, and blend on full power for 30 seconds. Add the orange liqueur and blend again until cool.

Pour the mousse into glasses. Cover each glass with a layer of clingfilm and allow to set in the fridge for a minimum of 2 hours before serving.

Serve with Guernsey butter biscuits. (See page 212).

DARK CHOCOLATE MOUSSE WITH HEDGEROW TAYBERRIES & RASPBERRIES

Serves 6 – Note this recipe contains raw eggs.

INGREDIENTS:

450ml	Guernsey Dairy whipping cream
45g	Caster sugar
300g	Dark bitter chocolate couverture (70% cocoa solids)
25ml	Freshly squeezed orange juice
20g	Orange zest
3	Free range eggs
150g	Fresh tayberries
150g	Fresh raspberries
25ml	Dark rum

METHOD:

Chop the chocolate into small pieces. Heat the cream to scalding point in a large saucepan with the caster sugar and orange zest.

Place the chocolate in a liquidiser and pour the scalded cream over it. Blend together for 30-40 seconds. Add the eggs and the orange juice. Blend again until cool.

Pour the mousse into glasses, cover with clingfilm and allow to set in the refrigerator for a minimum of 2 hours before serving.

Gently wash and pat dry the freshly picked berries, sprinkle with a shot of dark rum and leave to macerate until ready to serve.

DARK CHOCOLATE TRUFFLE CAKE

Serves 8-10 (1 x 27cm ring)

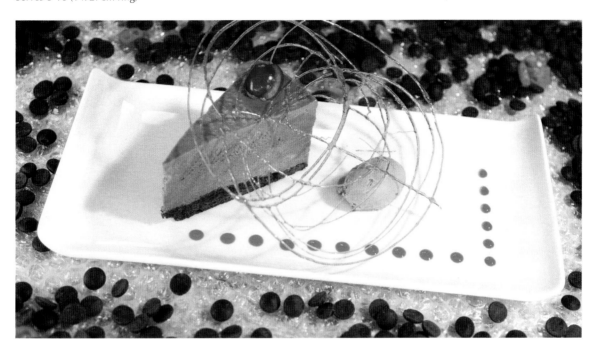

INGREDIENTS:

1	Thin layer of chocolate sponge (see page 207)
550ml	Guernsey Dairy whipping cream
450g	Dark bitter chocolate couverture (70% cocoa solids)
80ml	Water
80g	Caster sugar
80g	Liquid glucose
75ml	Stock syrup

METHOD:

Line the base of a 27cm diameter cake ring with a thin layer of chocolate sponge and drizzle with the stock syrup.

Chop the chocolate into small pieces and place in a large bowl and set aside.

Weigh the caster sugar on the scales, making a slight well in the middle. Fill it with the 80g of liquid glucose. This will prevent it from sticking to the weighing scales and you can simply pour both ingredients into a small saucepan. Add the water and bring to boiling point.

Boil rapidly for 2 minutes exactly before pouring onto the finely-chopped chocolate.

Whip the cream to soft peak stage. Using a whisk stir one third of the cream into the chocolate mixture then gently fold the remaining two thirds in using a spoon or spatula.

Pour into the cake ring and refrigerate until required.

Serve with dark chocolate & chilli ice cream. (See page 210).

Tony Leck's Pavilion on a Plate

FRUITY TEACAKE

1 x 20cm round

INGREDIENTS:

450g	Mixed dried fruits (cherries, prunes, sultanas, mixed peel)
335ml	Strong black tea
100ml	Orange juice
1	Orange (zest)
75g	Guernsey Dairy unsalted butter
335g	Self-raising flour
2	Free range eggs
25g	Demerara sugar

METHOD:

Place your choice of dried fruits in a bowl. Prepare hot black tea with your choice of tea or teabags and allow to infuse. Strain and pour the hot tea, orange juice and zest onto the dried fruit. Cover with cling film, then

leave for at least 3 hours or, preferably overnight. Pre-heat oven to 170°C, 340°F, Gas 4.

Grease and line the base of a 2lb loaf tin.

Beat together the butter and sugar until light white and creamy, then beat in the egg, followed by the sieved flour. Carefully stir through the fruit mixture. Spoon the mixture into the tin, then smooth over the surface with the back of a spoon. Sprinkle the top with a fine layer of demerara sugar. Bake for approximately 1 hour or until a skewer inserted into the centre comes out clean.

Leave to cool in the tin, then turn out, cut into slices and serve with tea and whipping cream.

This fruity teacake can be made up to one week in advance and stored in an airtight tin.

VICTORIA SANDWICH

Makes 2 x 20cm rounds

INGREDIENTS:

250g	Guernsey Dairy unsalted butter
250g	Caster sugar
1	Vanilla pod (split lengthways)
4	Free range eggs
250g	Self-raising flour
100g	Strawberry preserve
285ml	Guernsey Dairy whipping cream
25g	Caster or icing sugar

METHOD:

Pre-heat the oven to 190°C, 375°F, Gas 5. Lightly grease 2 x 20cm diameter sandwich tins and line the base of each with baking paper or dust with a little flour.

Place the butter into a large bowl together with seeds scraped from a vanilla pod and beat until soft. Add the sugar and continue beating until the mixture is light, white in colour and fluffy in texture. Beat the eggs in a separate bowl and pour through a fine sieve to avoid any fragments of egg shell in the finished product.

Gradually add the eggs, beating well after each addition.

Sieve the flour into the bowl and carefully fold it into the creamed mixture using a spatula.

Divide the mixture equally between the two prepared cake/sandwich tins, spread the mixture evenly and bake for 30-40 minutes until risen and springy to the touch. The sponge will slightly shrink away from the sides of the tins.

Remove from oven and allow to cool for 5 minutes in the tins upside down. This will allow steam to help release the sponges from the tins. Set aside on a wire rack and leave to cool completely.

When cool, place one of the sponges upside down and spread evenly with jam. Whisk the whipping cream together with a sprinkle of caster sugar and spread this over the jam, top with the second cake and sprinkle sugar over the top before serving.

For an alternative dish, substitute the jam and cream filling with lemon curd. (See page 208).

FRESH CHERRY SCONES

Serves 12-16

INGREDIENTS:

450g	Plain flour
140g	Guernsey Dairy unsalted butter
100g	Caster sugar
2	Free range eggs
30g	Baking powder
100g	Fresh cherries (stoned)
125ml	Guernsey Dairy milk (amount of milk will depend upon moisture content of cherries)
100g	Cherry preserve
150ml	Guernsey Dairy whipping cream
15g	Icing sugar

METHOD:

Sieve together the flour and baking powder. Lightly rub into this the caster sugar and diced butter until it is the consistency of ground almonds. Make a well in the centre of the mixture and lightly mix in the milk and beaten eggs.

Do not add all the liquid as flours vary in the amount of liquid they absorb.

De-stone the fresh cherries and add to the dough.

Lightly dust the work surface and roll out the dough with a rolling pin or simply flatten with your hands to approximately 2.5cm deep.

Do not over work or over mix the dough.

Cut rounds out using a pastry cutter and place on a baking sheet before baking at 220°C, 425°F, Gas 7 for 15 minutes.

The scones can be either left plain, sprinkled with sugar or brushed with egg yolk before baking, depending on your preferred finish.

Once baked allow to cool before serving with cream, jam, or both.

CARROT CAKE WITH ORANGE CREAM FILLING

Serves 10 (1 x 30cm ring)

INGREDIENTS:

850g	Soft brown sugar
4	Free range eggs
300ml	Corn oil
1	Vanilla pod (split)
850g	Grated carrot
425g	Wholemeal flour
285g	Flaked almonds
½ tsp	Salt
2 tsp	Ground cinnamon
2 tsp	Baking powder
	Walnut halves

Orange cream filling:

300g	Soft cream cheese
80g	Icing sugar
30g	Fine orange zest
30ml	Orange juice
1	Vanilla pod (split)
50g	Walnut or pecan nut halves

METHOD:

Peel and finely grate the carrots.

Split the vanilla pod and using a cook's knife, scrape out all the little seeds.

In a mixing bowl whisk together the soft brown sugar, vanilla seeds and eggs until light in texture. Gradually add the corn oil until all is incorporated.

Next sieve together the wholemeal flour, ground cinnamon, salt, and baking powder and set aside.

Add the grated carrot and flaked almonds to the egg mixture and mix well. Finally, fold the sieved dry ingredients into the above and mix lightly. Place into a greased cake ring and bake at 165°C, 330°F, Gas 4 until golden in colour and when a knife or skewer is inserted and comes away clean.

Remove from oven and allow to cool.

Whilst cooling, prepare the filling by scraping the seeds from the vanilla pod. Whisk these together with the finely-grated orange zest, icing sugar and soft cream cheese. Adjust consistency with freshly-squeezed orange juice.

Once cool, split cake into two with a serrated knife and spread the filling generously. Dust the cake with icing sugar and top with more cream filling and walnut or pecan halves.

For alternative flavours, try using grated parsnips with ginger or beetroot with a little horseradish.

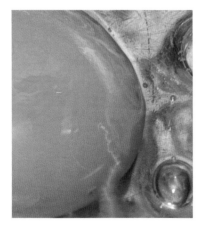

TRADITIONAL GUERNSEY GÂCHE

Serves 2 x loaf tins

INGREDIENTS:

550g	Plain flour
200g	Wholemeal flour
250g	Guernsey Dairy unsalted butter
125ml	Guernsey Dairy milk
30g	Caster sugar
1	Small apple (peeled, cored and diced)
2	Free range eggs
125g	Candied citrus peel
75g	Sultanas
60g	Fresh yeast
	Pinch of salt, ground cinnamon and nutmeg

METHOD:

Pre-heat the oven to 180°C, 350°F, Gas 4.

Peel, core and dice the apple finely, wash the sultanas and candied peel and dry thoroughly.

Mix the plain and wholemeal flour together with the ground spices.

Cream the butter with the caster sugar, add the beaten eggs and mix into this the dried ingredients to create a dough.

Warm the milk to blood temperature and add the yeast. Mix together and add a pinch of salt.

Combine the liquid with the dough and knead well as for bread, adding the dried fruits and diced apple.

Cover the dough with a cloth and leave to prove for 2 hours or until the dough has doubled in size. Knock back the dough and knead again before placing in a loaf tin.

Allow the dough to prove again and, when increased in volume, bake for approximately 1 hour until golden. Test with a skewer – it should be clean when removed.

Allow to cool on a baking rack before slicing and serving with Guernsey Dairy butter. Alternatively serve toasted like a teacake.

Any leftovers can be sliced and used in other dishes such as Guernsey Gâche 'n' Butter pudding. (See page 166).

CASTEL FARM EGGS

For me eggs are the ultimate convenience food. They arrive hygienically wrapped, are versatile, easy to cook and waste free. My only stipulation is that they should come from well cared-for hens and be as fresh as possible.

Castel Farm fulfils the criteria in every way. It is only a few miles from The Pavilion so it is not unheard of for the eggs to be still warm on arrival. There are restaurants on the island which are governed more by cost, importing their eggs from abroad, but my policy is always to support Guernsey suppliers.

Castel Farm is a producer which balances animal welfare with modern technology to meet the demands of its customers of whom I am just one – almost everyone on the island uses its eggs at some point during the year.

It has some 16,000 birds which are all free to roam on a rotational basis from the four hen houses with 'pop' doors that operate on electric timers. What I like about Castel Farm – apart from the freshness of its eggs – is that it encourages visitors, organising food tastings, farm visits and in-house promotions.

Its hens produce more than 14,000 eggs every day – they lay in the morning and are delivered in the afternoon. You can't get fresher than that.

"Our birds are Brown Shavers," said operations manager, Kevin Sorrell, a Londoner who has made Guernsey his home. "Some chicken breeds can be quite feisty but these are good-natured and regular layers which is just as well because we sell all we produce."

All aspects of the business are undertaken by the team, including engineering development and hen house construction, packaging design and marketing material as well as environmental issues including waste control and energy consumption. They are keen promoters of the island's fresh produce, regularly participating in Taste Guernsey events

BEEF STOCK

(1 litre)

INGREDIENTS:

2kg	Beef bones or beef shin
350g	Carrot (peeled)
1	Stick celery
1	Leek (washed and chopped)
1	Onion (chopped)
1	Bulb garlic
50g	Tomato purée
250g	Overripe tomatoes
3.5ltr	Water
1	Bay leaf
10g	Fresh thyme sprigs
20g	Fresh parsley stalks
25ml	Vegetable oil

METHOD:

Roughly chop the beef bones and vegetables into fairly evenly sized pieces.

Heat a large roasting tray in a pre-heated oven at 200°C, 400°F, Gas 6.

Add the oil and return the roasting tray to the oven for 5 minutes so that the oil becomes very hot. Add the beef bones and vegetables and cook until browned all over, slightly caramelised, stirring occasionally with a spatula. Leave to roast for at least one hour before draining through a colander to remove any excess fat.

Transfer these ingredients to a large saucepan or casserole dish and cover with the water. Add the Bay leaf and thyme before bringing to boiling point, skin the surface of any fat and / or scum which may rise to the top and simmer very gently for approximately 3-4 hours.

Add the remaining herbs and simmer for a further thirty minutes.

Pour the liquid through a fine sieve and either use immediately or keep the stock refrigerated and use within a couple of days. Once the stock has cooled, remove any layer of fat from the top prior to using. Reheat the stock and reduce in volume by half. The stock can be frozen for later use.

For lamb stock, substitute the beef bones with lamb bones.

BROWN CHICKEN STOCK

(1 litre)

INGREDIENTS:

1.5kg	Chicken wings
300g	Carrot (peeled)
1	Stick celery
1	Leek (washed and chopped)
1	Onion (chopped)
1	Bulb garlic
5	White peppercorns
2ltr	Water
1	Bay leaf
10g	Fresh thyme sprigs
20g	Fresh parsley stalks
25ml	Vegetable oil

METHOD:

Roughly chop the vegetables into fairly evenly sized pieces.

Heat a large roasting tray in a pre-heated oven at 200°C, 400°F, Gas 6.

Add the oil and return the roasting tray to the oven for 5 minutes so that the oil becomes very hot. Add the chicken wings and vegetables and cook until the wings are brown all over and the vegetables begin to slightly caramelise, stirring occasionally with a spatula. Drain the caramelised vegetables and chicken wings through a colander to remove any excess fat.

Transfer these ingredients to a large saucepan or casserole dish and cover with the water. Add the Bay leaf and thyme before bringing to boiling point and simmering gently for approximately 2 hours.

Add the remaining herbs and simmer for a further 30 minutes.

Pour the liquid through a fine sieve and either use immediately or keep the stock refrigerated and use within a couple of days. Once the stock has cooled, remove any layer of fat from the top prior to using. The stock can be frozen for later use.

For pork stock substitute the chicken wings for a pork trotter or pork hock.

VEGETABLE STOCK

(1 litre)

INGREDIENTS:

1	Carrot (peeled)
1	Stick celery
1	Leek (washed and chopped)
1	Fennel bulb (chopped)
1	Onion (chopped)
1	Bulb garlic
100ml	White wine
1ltr	Water
1	Bay leaf
20g	Fresh tarragon stalks
10g	Fresh dill
5g	Fresh thyme sprigs
20g	Fresh chervil
20g	Fresh parsley stalks
½	Lemon
1	Star anise

METHOD:

Roughly chop the vegetables into fairly evenly sized pieces.

Place the vegetables into a large saucepan or casserole dish and cover with the water. Add the bay leaf and thyme before bringing to boiling point and simmering gently for approximately 10 minutes.

Add the remaining herbs and simmer for a further 5 minutes.

Add the lemon together with the white wine and remove from the heat source and allow to cool.

Once cooled, pour the liquid through a fine sieve and either use immediately or keep the stock refrigerated and use within a couple of days.

The stock can be frozen for later use.

FISH STOCK

(1 litre)

INGREDIENTS:

750g	Good quality white fish bones such as sole, brill or plaice
20ml	Olive oil
1	Fennel bulb (chopped)
1	Onion (chopped)
100ml	White wine
2	Bay leaves
20g	Fresh tarragon stalks
10g	Fresh thyme sprigs
20g	Fresh chervil
20g	Fresh parsley stalks
5	Whole white peppercorns

METHOD:

Chop the fish bones into fairly even sizes and wash under cold water.

Heat the olive oil in a large saucepan or casserole dish and add the drained fish bones. Add the chopped fennel and onion together with the white wine and cover with a lid. Cook for 2-3 minutes until the wine has reduced to almost dry.

Cover with cold water and bring to the boil, skim any grease that may have risen to the top and add the fresh herbs together with the peppercorns.

Reduce the heat and simmer very gently for 20 minutes.

Allow the stock to cool with the bones still in before passing through a fine sieve; take care not to disturb any sediment in the base of the saucepan or casserole dish.

The stock will keep for a couple of day refrigerated or can be frozen for use at a later stage.

PARSLEY SAUCE

INGREDIENTS:

25g	Guernsey butter
30g	Plain flour
500ml	Guernsey milk
75g	Parsley
1	Chopped shallot
	Salt
	Pepper

METHOD:

Heat the milk together with the finely-chopped shallot and picked parsley stalks. Allow the milk to infuse. Melt the butter in a heavy-based saucepan. Add the sieved flour to make a roux. Gradually stir in the infused milk and cook gently for 20 minutes. Pass through a fine chinois or sieve. Add the chopped parsley and adjust seasoning to taste.

HERM ISLAND OYSTER KETCHUP

It's well worth making a job lot of this so you'll always have some to hand in the store cupboard. Try it as a condiment to underpin flavours, or use it in place of anchovy essence.

INGREDIENTS:

12	Oysters
50g	Anchovies (drained of oil)
1	Shallot (finely diced)
1	Lemon (juice and zest)
75ml	Dry white wine
95ml	Rocquette cider
½ tsp	Ground mace
½ tsp	Ground cloves

METHOD:

Open the oysters and place in a saucepan together with any liquor from the oysters. Add the drained anchovies, dry white wine, cider and lemon, bring to boil and simmer for 30 minutes.

Add the shallot and ground spices. Simmer for a further 10 minutes before straining through a fine muslin cloth into sterilized preserving jars and seal tightly.

Sterilize the jars by immersing them in hot water for 15 minutes or longer at 80°C, 180°F.

Store in a cool area, preferably refrigerated, until required.

FORT GREY TORTEVAL BLUE CHEESE SAUCE

INGREDIENTS:

450ml	Guernsey Dairy milk
1	Small onion
1	Bay leaf
1	Clove
60g	Guernsey butter
60g	Plain flour
25ml	Port
125g	Fort Grey cheese
Pinch	Freshly grated nutmeg
	Sea salt
	Freshly ground black pepper

METHOD:

Peel the onion and stud the bay leaf to the onion with the clove.

Place the milk in a heavy based saucepan with the studded onion, add the nutmeg and bring to boiling point, reduce heat and simmer to allow the flavours to infuse.

In another saucepan, melt the butter. When it begins to froth add the flour and stir well to form a roux. Strain the hot milk and gradually add the milk to the roux a little at a time, stirring continuously to prevent any lumps forming. Once all the milk is incorporated, simmer the sauce for 20 minutes over a low heat, stirring occasionally. Grate the Fort Grey blue cheese and add to the sauce together with the port, strain the sauce through a fine chinois or sieve, season to taste and serve.

Tony Leck's Pavilion on a Plate

MAYONNAISE

INGREDIENTS:

6	Free range egg yolks
2 tbsp	Dijon mustard
2 tbsp	White wine vinegar
300ml	Olive oil
900ml	Vegetable or sunflower oil
1	Lemon (juice)
	Sea salt
	Freshly-ground white peppercorns

METHOD:

Blend the egg yolks, mustard and lemon juice together in a food processor until well combined. Gradually add the oil to the egg mixture in a steady stream whilst the processor is still running. Continue until it is all incorporated.

Adjust the seasoning to taste using sea salt and freshly-ground white peppercorns.

If the mayonnaise is too thick adjust the consistency with a little water, or lemon if more acidity is needed.

RED BELL PEPPER MAYONNAISE

INGREDIENTS:

4	Red bell peppers
6	Free range egg yolks
2 tbsp	Dijon mustard
2 tbsp	Lemon juice
700ml	Vegetable or sunflower oil
	Sea salt
	Freshly ground black peppercorns

METHOD:

Place the peppers either in a hot oven or under a grill until the skin scorches.

Remove from the heat and seal inside a plastic bag. This will allow the peppers to sweat, making the removal of the skin easier. Skin and de-seed.

Blend the egg yolks, mustard and lemon juice together in a food processor until well combined. Gradually add the oil to the egg mixture in a steady stream whilst the processor is still running until it is all incorporated. Add the flesh of the red peppers and continue to blend. Adjust the seasoning to taste with sea salt and freshly ground black peppercorns.

If the mayonnaise is too thick adjust the consistency with a little water, or lemon juice if it requires a little more acidity.

Mayonnaise is a very versatile sauce. It can be enriched with an array of flavours from various herbs through to zesty fruits or with peppers, as above.

Always use quality eggs from a reliable source that have been stored correctly.

Mayonnaise is best made from neutral unsaturated oils such as vegetable or sunflower. Olive oil is too strong and will taste bitter.

PICCALILLI

INGREDIENTS:

2 tsp	English mustard
2 tsp	Ground ginger
1 tsp	Ground turmeric
175g	Soft brown sugar
750ml	White wine vinegar
50ml	Lemon juice
30g	Corn flour
250g	Sea salt
1.5kg	Your choice of vegetables
	Florets of cauliflower
	Button onions
	Diced carrot
	Diced cucumber
	Diced peppers
	Diced courgettes

METHOD:

Any combination of vegetables may be used, so pick your personal favourites.

Prepare the vegetables, mix with sea salt and set aside for a day. Rinse the vegetables thoroughly, drain well and pat dry.

Put the English mustard, ground turmeric, ground ginger and soft brown sugar together in a saucepan with the white wine vinegar.

Add the vegetables, bring to boil and simmer gently for 15-20 minutes depending upon the vegetables chosen – do not overcook. Put in sterilized jars leaving 5-10cms at the top.

Reheat the cooking liquid and bring to the boil. Dissolve the corn flour with the lemon juice and add to the boiling liquid. Boil for 3-4 minutes and strain through a sieve over the bottled vegetables.

Cover and seal the jars. Cool and leave for several days before serving.

HOLLANDAISE SAUCE

INGREDIENTS:

250g	Guernsey Dairy butter
4	Free range egg yolks
75ml	White wine vinegar
½	Shallot (finely diced)
½	Lemon (juice and zest)
	Freshly ground blackpeppercorns
	Salt

METHOD:

Melt the butter carefully and discard the milk solids which will sink to the bottom.

Place the vinegar in a saucepan together with the chopped shallot, zest of lemon and a little cracked black pepper. Raise the heat and reduce the vinegar by half in volume then set aside to cool slightly.

In a large stainless steel bowl whisk the egg yolks over a water bath or bain-marie until they are light and white and double in volume. Do not allow the water bath to boil as this may result in the eggs being scrambled. Add the reduced vinegar, discarding the chopped shallot. Slowly add the melted butter a little at a time by whisking into the egg mixture until all is incorporated. Add a squeeze of lemon juice to taste; this will also thin the sauce slightly. Season with salt and pepper to taste.

BRAISED RED CABBAGE

INGREDIENTS:

500g	Red cabbage
150ml	Chicken stock (see page 189)
2	Medium cooking apples
1	Onion
	Chicken stock
50g	Guernsey butter
150ml	Red wine
25ml	Red wine vinegar
75ml	Redcurrant jelly
50g	Demerara sugar
80g	Sultanas
1	Cinnamon stick (snapped in half)
2-3	Bay leaves
4	Whole cloves
	Sea salt
	Freshly ground black pepper

METHOD:

Prepare the cabbage by cutting into four quarters before shredding each piece finely.

Add the chopped onion, sultanas and sugar and set aside to infuse overnight.

Melt the butter in a large saucepan and add the onion mixture, stirring occasionally and season.

Peel, core and chop the apples into the saucepan along with the vinegar, red wine, redcurrant jelly and spices.

Cook for approximately 5 minutes before adding some stock to barely cover the cabbage. Cover with a lid and braise slowly in a moderate oven or over a very gentle heat on top of the stove until the cabbage is tender.

Remove the cinnamon stick before transferring to storage jars.

Braised cabbage stores well in the refrigerator and is an ideal vegetable dish for the winter months, though remember when seasoning that the spices will mature with time.

PICKLED RED CABBAGE

INGREDIENTS:

500g	Red cabbage
300ml	Red wine
150ml	Malt vinegar
150ml	Balsamic vinegar
300g	Demerara sugar
	Whole cloves
1	Cinnamon stick (snapped in half)
3-4	Bay leaves
60g	Sea salt
	Freshly ground black pepper

METHOD:

Pickled cabbage is best prepared at least a day in advance.

Quarter and finely shred the cabbage. Place in a large colander or bowl and sprinkle well with the sea salt. Leave for 2-3 hours, allowing the deep rich ruby red colour to come alive.

Rinse the cabbage with cold water and pat dry with a paper towel.

In a large saucepan, bring the red wine to boiling point together with the two vinegars and demerara sugar. Simmer and allow to reduce in volume by approximately half.

Grind together the cinnamon stick, bay leaves, black pepper and whole cloves in a pestle and mortar or a blender if time is lacking. Add the spices to the reduced liquid and allow to infuse for approximately 10 minutes.

Re-boil the liquid, pass through a sieve and pour onto the shredded cabbage. While still hot, place in suitable storage jars. Seal the jars when cool. Refrigerate the following day until required.

RED ONION JAM

INGREDIENTS:

500g	Red onions
175ml	Red wine
50ml	Sherry vinegar
150ml	Balsamic vinegar
150g	Demerara sugar
100g	Guernsey Dairy butter
30g	Unbleached sea salt
	Freshly ground black peppercorns

METHOD:

Prepare the onions by peeling and slicing very thinly. Place in a large stainless steel bowl and mix well with sea salt, freshly ground black peppercorns and the sugar.

Set aside for 2 hours.

Heat the butter in a large saucepan until it begins to foam. Add the onions just before the butter begins to brown and stir well, reducing the heat slightly.

Continue to stir regularly until the onions are almost softened and cooked. At this stage add the sherry vinegar, balsamic vinegar and red wine.

Simmer over a gentle heat for up to 1 hour. Adjust the seasoning and set aside until required.

This jam can be bottled and stored, preferably in a refrigerator.

Tony Leck's Pavilion on a Plate

YORKSHIRE PUDDING

Serves 6

INGREDIENTS:

225g	Plain flour (sieved)
8	Free range eggs
600ml	Guernsey Dairy milk
1 tsp	Malt vinegar
50ml	Vegetable oil or beef dripping
	Sea salt
	Freshly ground black pepper

METHOD:

Place the sieved flour and eggs together in a bowl with some salt and pepper. Whisk together until smooth. Gradually stir in the milk and beat well until any lumps have disappeared and the batter is the consistency of thick cream. Whisk in a teaspoon of malt vinegar and pour through a sieve.

Allow the batter to 'rest' for at least 30 minutes or preferably overnight in the refrigerator.

Pre-heat the oven to 220°C, 425°F, Gas 7.

Place a Yorkshire pudding tray on a slightly larger tray and put in the oven to heat through. When hot, put a little beef dripping or vegetable oil on to the tray, pour in the batter and put back in the oven to bake for approximately 25-30 minutes.

TOAD IN THE HOLE

Serves 6

INGREDIENTS:

12	Porky's sausages
50g	Bayeux mustard
20g	Fresh Guernsey thyme (snipped)
20ml	Beef dripping or vegetable oil

METHOD:

Prepare the Yorkshire pudding batter as above and leave to rest. Sauté the sausages gently in a non-stick frying pan with a splash of dripping or vegetable oil until evenly coloured and almost cooked through.

Remove the sausages from the pan and roll in a little grain mustard.

Place the sausages on a baking tray or in an earthenware dish and pour over the Yorkshire pudding batter. Bake in a pre-heated oven for 25-30 minutes.

DAUPHINOISE POTATOES

INGREDIENTS:

300ml	Guernsey Dairy whipping cream
300ml	Guernsey Dairy milk
4	Crushed garlic bulbs
1	Onion (finely sliced)
1kg	Maris Piper potatoes
2	Bay leaves
50g	Guernsey Dairy butter
	Sea salt
	Freshly ground black pepper

METHOD:

Pour the cream and milk into a heavy-based saucepan. Warm along with the crushed garlic, bay leaves and sliced onion. Slowly bring to scalding point before removing from the heat and allowing the flavours to infuse.

Peel the potatoes and slice very thinly using a mandolin. Strain the milk mixture and set aside. Layer the sliced potatoes in an ovenproof dish or saucepan. Season each layer of potatoes with salt and pepper and a sprinkling of the cooked sliced onion and garlic, finishing off with a layer of potato. When all the potatoes are layered, pour over the infused creamy milk.

Place little knobs of the butter over the top and place in the oven to cook for approximately 1½ hours or until the top is golden and the centre is tender when tested with a skewer or a knife. Serve immediately.

Tony Leck's Pavilion on a Plate

TRADITIONAL GUERNSEY SAVOURY BISCUITS

INGREDIENTS:

350g	Plain flour
100g	Wholemeal flour
250g	Guernsey Dairy unsalted butter
185-200ml	Guernsey Dairy milk
15g	Caster sugar
15g	Salt
30g	Fresh yeast
	Pinch of salt, ground cinnamon and nutmeg

METHOD:

Pre-heat the oven to 180°C, 350°F, Gas 4.

Cream together the butter, yeast and sugar

Warm the milk to blood temperature and add to the yeast, sugar and butter mix.

Mix the plain and wholemeal flour together with the ground spices.

Add the dry ingredients to the liquid and knead well, as for bread.

Cover the dough with a cloth and leave to prove for 1½ hours or until the dough has doubled in size.

Knock back the dough and knead again on a lightly floured work surface before forming into round shapes.

Place on a lightly greased baking sheet, allow the dough to prove again and, when increased in volume, bake for approximately 20 minutes until golden.

Serve with traditional Guernsey bean jar or freshly prepared soup.

OATMEAL DIGESTIVE BISCUITS

INGREDIENTS:

225g	Wholemeal flour
225g	Oatmeal
1 tsp	Bicarbonate of soda
20g	Demerara sugar
80g	Guernsey Dairy butter
15ml	Guernsey Dairy milk
¼	Lemon (juice)
	Pinch of salt (optional)

METHOD:

Use a medium cut oatmeal, f none is available grind rough oatmeal in a blender.

Place the sieved flour, bicarbonate of soda, oatmeal, sugar and salt if using (salt is optional depending whether you have included salted or unsalted butter in the recipe) in a large bowl with the lemon juice. Rub the butter in until the mixture is crumble-like in texture. Add the milk and mix to create a dough. Divide the dough into smaller batches and roll each out with a rolling pin to approximately 3mm thick, lightly dusting the work surface as you go. Cut out discs with a 7cm diameter pastry cutter. Prick each biscuit with a fork to prevent the biscuits rising whilst baking – this also helps to bake them evenly.

Transfer the biscuits to baking trays and allow to rest for 20-30 minutes before baking at 180°C, 350°F, Gas 4 for 12-15 minutes until the biscuits are an even golden brown colour. Cool on a rack prior to serving.

Tony Leck's Pavilion on a Plate

GUERNSEY HONEY & OATMEAL BISCUITS

INGREDIENTS:

450g	Plain flour
2½ level tsp	Bicarbonate of soda
450g	Demerara sugar
450g	Rolled porridge oats
450g	Unsalted Guernsey Dairy butter
5 tbsp	Dark rum
5 tbsp	Guernsey honey

METHOD:

Sieve together the flour and bicarbonate of soda.

Add the sugar and oats.

Melt the butter in a saucepan with the honey and dark rum over a gentle heat.

While still warm mix with the dry ingredients and shape into rounds.

Press down to biscuit shape and bake in a moderate oven at 165°C, 330°F, Gas 3-4 until golden.

GUERNSEY HONEY SNAPS

INGREDIENTS:

125g	Plain flour
250g	Caster sugar
1tsp	Ground ginger
125g	Unsalted Guernsey butter (softened)
125g	Guernsey honey

METHOD:

Sieve together the flour and ginger.

In a bowl, cream together the sugar and butter until light and fluffy in appearance.

Warm the honey slightly and add gradually to the butter and sugar mixture. Stir in the sieved flour and ground ginger.

Roll the mixture into a long sausage 3-4cm in diameter and wrap tightly in clingfilm.

Chill in the refrigerator, preferably overnight.

Remove the clingfilm and cut off slices approximately 5mm thick. Place slices on a prepared baking tray, spacing them out as they will spread when baking.

Pre-heat the oven and bake until golden at 180°C, 350°F, Gas 4 for 7-8 minutes.

Remove from the oven and allow to cool slightly before removing from the baking tray and shaping as desired.

If the biscuits cool too quickly to work with, simply return to the oven for a minute to re-heat.

Guernsey honey snaps become crisp as they cool and will stay crisp provided they are stored in an airtight container.

Additional flavours can be created by using infused honeys such as lavender.

To prepare traditional ginger snaps simply replace the Guernsey honey with golden syrup and add one teaspoon of ground ginger.

Add a teaspoon of ground cinnamon or allspice for an alternative flavoured biscuit.

Tony Leck's Pavilion on a Plate

RASPBERRY JAM

INGREDIENTS:

500g	Fresh raspberries
500g	Jam sugar (with pectin)
	Juice of half a lemon

METHOD:

Wash and gently pat dry the fruit. Place in a heavy-based saucepan with the sugar sprinkled over the top, followed by the lemon juice.

Leave to marinate for 30 minutes or until the fruits have started to bleed.

Dissolve the sugar over a low heat. Stop stirring the contents of the pan once the jam starts to boil.

Cook to 107°C, 225°F before transferring to a clean container and leave to cool before storing.

RED BERRY COULIS

INGREDIENTS:

275g	Fresh red berries
275g	Icing sugar
1	Lemon or lime (juice)

METHOD:

Wash and gently pat dry the berries and place in a bowl with the sugar.

Leave to macerate for 30 minutes or until the fruit has started to bleed.

Place the fruit, any juice and sugar into a food processor and purée.

Pass through a fine sieve. Adjust the seasoning with a little squeeze of lemon or lime juice if required.

Set aside in a refrigerator until required.

WALNUT BREAD

INGREDIENTS:

1.5kg	Strong flour
2 tsp	Salt
75g	Yeast
175g	Guernsey Dairy butter
235g	Soft brown sugar
800ml	Guernsey Dairy milk
275ml	Warm water
450g	Chopped walnuts

METHOD:

Mix together the salt, yeast and water.

Warm the butter and blend with the milk. Stir into this the sugar and yeast mixture, then the flour and mix well. Add the chopped walnuts.

Lightly dust the work surface with a little extra flour if required and continue to knead well. At this stage you may need to add any remaining water, though do so cautiously. The amount of water required will depend upon the flour used, the humidity of your kitchen and the temperature of the ingredients. Do not beat aggressively with a machine dough hook as this will result in doughy, chewy bread! Continue to knead the dough for approximately 10 minutes. Cover with clingfilm and leave to rest for 45-50 minutes in a warm area of the kitchen (warm not hot!).

Return the dough to the work surface and lightly dust with a little flour. Knead the dough again for a further 5 minutes.

Shape into required sizes (loaves, rolls etc.) and place on baking trays. Cover with clingfilm and return to the warm area of the kitchen.

Allow to prove for approximately 45-60 minutes before placing in a hot oven.

After 5-10 minutes baking, spray the bread with a little water which will give the end result a better crust.

Loaves may take up to 30 minutes to bake depending upon size. To check if the loaves are ready, pick up the loaf and tap the bottom of it. A hollow sound indicates it is ready. Remove from the oven and place upon a cooling tray until ready to use.

Remember, warm water should not exceed blood temperature as this will kill the activity of the yeast.

SWEET SHORTCRUST PASTRY

INGREDIENTS:

450g	Plain flour (sieved)
250g	Guernsey Dairy unsalted butter (diced)
110g	Icing sugar
1	Free range egg
1	Vanilla pod (seeds)
	Lemon (zest) (optional)
	Small quantity of beaten egg

METHOD:

Place the cold butter, sieved flour, sugar and seeds scraped from a vanilla pod together in a food processor and blitz for a few seconds until a fine breadcrumb-like texture (the zest of one lemon, finely grated adds a refreshing flavour to the pastry). Do not overmix the pastry. Add the free range egg and, using the pulse button of your processor, carefully bind, being very careful not to overmix the pastry as this will result in a pastry that both shrinks when cooked and has a doughy texture when eaten.

Remove from the food processor and place on a layer of cling film. Flatten slightly to create more surface area and cover with more cling film. Place in the refrigerator for 20-30 minutes to allow the pastry to chill and rest, the end result will be an easier product to work with, also one that will not shrink when cooked.

For lining tarts; lightly dust the work surface with a little flour and roll the pastry into a circular shape approximately 2cm larger than your chosen pastry or tart ring.

Keep moving the pastry as you roll it, by turning it 90 degrees to prevent the glutens stretching in one direction.

Ideally, the pastry should be about 0.25cm thick. Roll onto the rolling pin before unrolling onto your chosen pastry ring, being careful not to break the pastry or stretch it too much.

Unroll the pastry and gently ease into the ring, avoiding any creases. Allow the pastry to hang over the top edge of the ring slightly. Prick the base of the ring with a fork to prevent the base from rising when baking and to ensure a crisp baked base to your pastry case. Allow to rest for a further 30 minutes before trimming any excess overhang of pastry with a sharp knife.

Pre-heat the oven to 200°C, 400°F, Gas 6.

Cut a large round disc of parchment or greaseproof paper. Carefully place this into the pastry case and fill with either baking beans or rice and bake for approximately 15 minutes until the pastry has set. Remove the beans and the paper and reduce the oven temperature to 160°C, 325°F, Gas 3. Bake for a further 5-10 minutes depending on the thickness of the pastry.

Remove the pastry case from the oven and, using a pastry brush, paint the inside of the pastry case with a beaten egg. Return to the oven for 2 minutes. This will help to retain crispness and prevent the base from becoming soggy when the filling is added.

VANILLA SPONGE

Makes 1 x 27cm diameter cake

INGREDIENTS:

6	Free range eggs
175g	Caster sugar
175g	Plain flour (sieved)
50g	Unsalted Guernsey butter
1	Vanilla pod (split lengthways and seeds scraped out)

This is a basic recipe that can be used to form the base of many gateaux, trifles and other desserts.

To prepare chocolate sponge simply replace 30g of plain flour with 30g of cocoa powder and sieve the two dry ingredients together.

To prepare coffee sponge simply replace 30g plain flour with 30g of freeze dried coffee.

Other flavours can be simply adapted by adding the zest of a lime, lemon or orange. If you only require a thin layer of sponge for a dessert, prepare the whole recipe, slice a layer off with a sharp serrated cook's knife, wrap the remainder in clingfilm and freeze until required. The addition of melted butter to this recipe not only improves flavour but also keeps the sponge moist for longer.

METHOD:

Pre-heat the oven to 200°C, 400°F, Gas 6

Line a 27cm diameter cake tin with baking parchment or greaseproof paper.

Place the sugar on a baking sheet lined with baking parchment or greaseproof paper and place in the oven for 3-4 minutes to warm through but not melting or beginning to caramelise.

Meanwhile, whisk the eggs in a bowl until they become light in texture. Add the warmed sugar and continue whisking until doubled in volume and light and creamy. Add the vanilla seeds and whisk a little more.

Lightly fold in the flour, mixing very gently, being careful not to knock out all the air in the mix.

Gently melt the butter and gently fold in.

Pour the mixture into the prepared tin and bake for 30-40 minutes.

To test the sponge is ready, insert a skewer which will come out clean when the sponge is cooked. Allow the sponge to cool for 5 minutes in the tin (this will create a little steam around the sponge, thus making it easier to release from the tin) before turning out onto a wire rack to cool.

STOCK SYRUP

INGREDIENTS:

400g	Caster sugar
350ml	Water
1	Lemon
1	Orange
50g	Liquid glucose

METHOD:

Wash the citrus fruits under warm water to remove any impurities. Cut the fruits in half, place in a saucepan, with the water, sugar and liquid glucose and slowly bring to boiling point, stirring occasionally. Simmer for 2-3 minutes. Skim the surface with a ladle if any impurities rise to the top and discard. Pour the syrup through a fine sieve and leave to cool before storing in a refrigerator.

The citrus fruits can be reserved for use in other dishes.

This stock will keep for up to two weeks if stored correctly.

The above recipe is for a basic stock syrup. Various spices may be added – cloves, cinnamon, juniper berries, Earl Grey tea, ginger etc.

LEMON CURD

INGREDIENTS:

2	Lemons (zest and juice)
250g	Unsalted Guernsey butter (cut into small pieces)
250g	Caster sugar
4	Free range eggs

METHOD:

Place the zest and juice of the fruit into a bowl over a pan of gently simmering water. Do not allow the base of the bowl to be in contact with the water. Add the butter to the bowl. Whisk the eggs slightly and sieve into the mixture to remove any white threads of egg.

Stir the mixture continuously over the water for 20 minutes or more, until the mixture thickens. Do not let it boil as it will curdle.

Remove from the heat when thickened and pour through a sieve into clean warm jars. Cover the jars immediately with waxed discs of paper and leave until cold. Seal the jars and store refrigerated until required.

Curds made of fruit, eggs, butter and sugar will not keep for ever. They are best eaten within a few weeks.

SLOE GIN

Sloe gin is perfect for warming on a cold day and is best made late September or during October. Allow the berries to fully ripen before picking. Traditionally, sloes were only picked after the first frosts of the forthcoming winter. Pick the berries during October, and the gin will be ready for Christmas and the New Year. Sloe gin can also add an extra depth to savoury dishes. Add it to the juices of a roasting tin to enhance gravies, pour over game birds when roasting or add to meats when marinating.

INGREDIENTS:

450g	Sloes
350g	Caster sugar
1 litre	Gin

METHOD:

Wash the sloes, remove the stalks and prick the berries all over with a sharp needle or cook's knife.

Pack tightly into an airtight container or preserving jar, laying alternate layers of berries and sugar. Pour on the gin and seal the preserving jars tight.

Set aside and store in a dark and cool place for 10-12 weeks. For the first couple of weeks, either shake or invert the jar on a daily basis. After this period reduce the frequency to once a week. The gin is ready when the colour resembles a quality Beaujolais.

Strain the gin through a muslin cloth into clean sterilized preserving jars or bottles and keep stored until required.

Sloe gin is best served in a warmed glass to release maximum flavour.

SLOE GIN CUSTARD

INGREDIENTS:

400ml	Guernsey Dairy whipping cream
100ml	Sloe gin
5	Free range egg yolks
120g	Caster sugar

METHOD:

Bring the whipping cream to scalding point.

Meanwhile, whisk together the caster sugar and free range egg yolks until light and white in colour.

Pour on the hot cream, return the mixture to a hot clean saucepan and cook over a gentle heat, stirring constantly until the sauce begins to thicken slightly and coats the back of a spoon. Do not allow the sauce to boil as this will curdle the eggs resulting in sweet scrambled eggs.

Add the sloe gin, pour through a fine sieve and serve immediately or allow to cool depending on your preference.

These recipes require an ice cream machine.

RASPBERRY ICE CREAM

INGREDIENTS:

500ml	Guernsey whipping cream
300g	Caster sugar
500ml	Raspberry purée

METHOD:

Technically this is not an ice cream recipe but more a water ice recipe made with cream in place of the water.

To prepare, simply purée freshly-picked raspberries and pass through a fine sieve.

In a saucepan bring the cream and sugar to scalding point and remove from heat.

Allow to cool. When chilled, add the puréed raspberries and proceed to churn in an ice cream machine.

This dish is at its best during summer months when there is an abundance of fresh fruit.

Other varieties can be prepared depending upon what fruits are in season. The sugar content of various fruits may vary slightly so adjust the amount of sugar you add accordingly.

DARK CHOCOLATE & CHILLI ICE CREAM

INGREDIENTS:

500ml	Guernsey milk
125g	Caster sugar
50g	Liquid glucose
100g	Dark bitter chocolate couverture (70% cocoa solids)
30g	Extra dark cocoa powder
50g	Chopped red chilli peppers

METHOD:

Place the milk, sugar, cocoa powder and liquid glucose together in a thick-bottomed saucepan and bring to the boil over a steady heat whilst stirring continuously with a whisk. Once at boiling point, simmer gently for several minutes until the cocoa powder has cooked out and the floury texture has gone.

Remove the pan from the heat and add the chopped chocolate couverture and chillies.

Stir once again with a whisk for a further 2 minutes before pouring through a fine sieve into a bowl. Allow to cool to room temperature then refrigerate.

Once cool pour into an ice cream machine and proceed to churn until frozen with a smooth texture.

NUTMEG ICE CREAM

INGREDIENTS:

500ml	Guernsey milk
125g	Caster sugar
6	Free range egg yolks
1	Whole nutmeg (finely grated)
100m	Guernsey whipping cream

METHOD:

Prepare in exactly the same way as for vanilla ice cream or the clove ice cream recipe.

Both the clove and nutmeg recipes are warming sensual flavours which marry well with winter desserts and puddings, though the different flavours and spices or herbs which can be incorporated into ice creams can stretch as far as the cook's imagination.

Nutmeg ice cream is also a wonderful accompaniment to a very simple yet traditional family-style dessert – the custard tart.

CLOVE ICE CREAM

A wonderful flavour ice cream which reminds me of the dentist's chair… only this is a recipe for pleasure not pain!

INGREDIENTS:

500ml	Guernsey milk
125g	Caster sugar
6	Free range egg yolks
8	Cloves
100ml	Guernsey whipping cream

METHOD:

Whisk together the egg yolks with half of the sugar in a bowl until white in colour and of a ribbon consistency.

Bring the milk to the boil with the remaining sugar. (Note: at this stage you would add split vanilla pods if making Crème Anglaise. It's the same basic recipe but with cloves instead of vanilla).

Once at boiling point pour onto the egg yolk/sugar mixture, whisking continuously.

Return the mixture to the pan and heat gently, stirring constantly until the custard is thickening slightly and will coat the back of a spoon.

Heat to 80°C, 160°F but it's important you do not boil as this will result in something resembling sweet scrambled eggs!

Pass the sauce through a fine sieve into a bowl and allow to cool, stirring occasionally to prevent a skin forming.

When cold, pour the sauce into an ice cream churner and begin to freeze.

When the sauce is beginning to chill and slightly thicken, add the remaining whipping cream and continue to churn for a further 10-15 minutes. Chill before serving.

BASIL ICE CREAM

INGREDIENTS:

500ml	Guernsey milk
125g	Caster sugar
6	Free range egg yolks
100m	Guernsey cream
250g	Freshly picked Guernsey basil leaves

METHOD:

Boil the milk. Wash the freshly-picked basil leaves and add to the milk at boiling point. Allow to infuse for 10 minutes before proceeding to make the sauce Anglaise.

With a hand blender beat the mixture until combined.

Cook as for basic vanilla ice cream, (see page 213).

Pass through a fine sieve and allow to cool prior to churning in an ice cream machine.

Basil ice cream eats well either on its own or with lightly-peppered fresh Guernsey strawberries and a splash of aged balsamic vinegar or a citrus-scented dessert.

GUERNSEY BUTTER BISCUITS

These biscuits are ideal served with any of the ice cream recipes.

Guernsey butter biscuits:

2	Free range egg whites
40g	Plain flour (sieved)
50g	Icing sugar (sieved)
60g	Unsalted Guernsey butter
100ml	Strawberry sauce or strawberry coulis (see page 204)

Guernsey butter biscuits:

Whisk together the egg whites with the icing sugar, add the flour and mix to a paste. Melt the butter and add to the paste to make a batter.

Set aside this batter in the refrigerator to allow to rest for 30 minutes.

Then spread the batter thinly onto lightly greased baking sheets or onto baking mats in round shapes.

Bake at 165°C, 330°F or Gas 3-4 for 3-4 minutes until a light golden colour. Whilst still hot, remove from the trays and mould over an upturned cup or a ramekin dish to create a basket shape. The paste will set crisp immediately on cooling.

VANILLA ICE CREAM

INGREDIENTS:

500ml	Guernsey Dairy milk
100ml	Guernsey Dairy whipping cream
125g	Caster sugar
6	Free range egg yolks
2	Vanilla pods (split lengthways)

METHOD:

The basis of many ice creams is *crème Anglaise* or English custard.

To prepare this basic sauce, whisk together the egg yolks with half of the sugar in a bowl until white in colour and of a ribbon consistency.

Bring the milk to the boil with the remaining sugar and split vanilla pods.

Once at boiling point pour onto the egg yolk/sugar mixture, whisking continuously.

Return the mixture to the pan and heat gently, stirring constantly until the custard is slightly thickening and will coat the back of a spoon. Heat to 86°C, 185°F.

Do not boil, as this will result into something resembling sweet scrambled eggs!

Pass the sauce through a fine sieve into a bowl and allow to cool, stirring occasionally to prevent a skin forming.

When cold, pour the sauce into an ice cream churner and begin to freeze.

When the sauce is beginning to chill and slightly thicken, add the remaining Guernsey whipping cream and continue to churn for a further 10-15 minutes.

SULTANA CUSTARD

INGREDIENTS:

500ml	Guernsey Dairy milk
100ml	Guernsey Dairy whipping cream
125g	Caster sugar
6	Free range egg yolks
1	Vanilla pod (split lengthways)
50g	Sultanas

METHOD:

Prepare a basic *crème Anglaise* or English custard as per vanilla ice cream (above) by whisking together the egg yolks with half of the sugar in a bowl until white in colour and of a ribbon consistency.

Bring the milk and cream to the boil with the remaining sugar, sultanas and split vanilla pod.

Once at boiling point pour onto the egg yolk/sugar mixture, whisking continuously.

Return the mixture to the pan and heat gently, stirring constantly until the custard is slightly thickening and will coat the back of a spoon. Heat to 86°C, 185°F taking care not to boil the sauce.

ALLY CLARK

Ally Clark took the long road from Aberdeen, Scotland to the island of Guernsey.

In an earlier life as an economist and later an IT consultant, he lived in London. They upped sticks, when his wife, also an economist, was sent by her company to the Cayman Islands. The move coincided with his realisation that the time was right to take up photography professionally.

Photography had always been a passion of his. While Ally is largely self-taught, he studied Photography on a part-time basis along with History of Art. But it was the time he spent in the Cayman Islands that really inspired him and helped to uncover his true talent.

A subsequent move to Guernsey introduced him to a whole new range of photo opportunities. Indeed, he firmly believes that the unique light in Guernsey has helped to produce some of his best work so far.

Ally has been contributing to a number of photographic agencies for several years but his big break came when he was selected as an exciting new talent in Who's Who in Visual Art – 100 Fine Art Photographers published by Art Domain in 2011. Many of his images now appear on book covers and in magazines. His work is influenced by American photographers of the 1960s and he has exhibited in the Cayman Islands, London and at The Guernsey Festival of Performing Arts.

Ally met Tony shortly after arriving on the island at a St Andrew's evening event. He was delighted to accept the commission for this book, and not a little surprised how it has revealed the island to him in ways that he didn't expect. Over many months he was called on to create images of everything from smiling faces to delicious food and, of course, the beautiful and delightfully photogenic Guernsey cows.

RECIPE INDEX

INDEX **PAGE**

A

Ale 'n' Onion Soup 24
Almond, Fig Tart 170
Almond Sponge filling 170
Apple & Calvados Baba 151
Apple & Walnut Tart with Torteval Blue Cheese Sauce,
  Baby Spinach & Walnut Salad 50
Arctic Roll, Raspberry with Summer Berries 156
Asparagus 44, 55, 70, 74
Asparagus Spears, Poached Free Range Egg, Ham Croquette 44

B

Baba, Apple & Calvados 151
Baby Spinach Risotto (with Poached Haddock) 84
Baby Spinach & Walnut Salad 50, 51
Baked Castel Farm Eggs with Baby Spinach
  & Torteval Blue Cheese Sauce 51
Baked Custard Tart with Nutmeg 152
Baked 'Frie d'or' in a box 30
Barbequed Rocquette Cider Sauce 116, 120
Basil Ice Cream 150, 212
Bayeux Mustard Dressing (with Ham Hock Terrine) 39
Bayeux Mustard Sauce (with Loin of Pork) 123
Bean Jar, Traditional 112
Beef Brisket, (Slow-Roasted with Chasseur Sauce) 128
Beef 'n' 'Cynful Ale' Pie 132
Beef Stock 188
Beer Batter 100
Beetroot, Orange & Hazelnut Salad, Rocket & Parmesan Salad 36
Beetroot, Parsley & Lemon Butter 76
Beetroot Risotto with Soft Goats Cheese 56
Beetroot Stock 36, 56
Bell Pepper (Red) Mayonnaise 66, 98, 194
Belly Pork, Slow-Roasted 120
Biscuits, Guernsey Butter 150, 212
Biscuits, Honey & Oatmeal 202
Biscuits, Oatmeal Digestive 201
Biscuits, Traditional Guernsey (savoury) 201
Bisque, Crab 34
Black Pudding Bonbons 72
Blue Cheese Bonbons 130
Blue Cheese Dip 59
Blue Cheese Sauce 50, 51, 193
Boiled Ham with White Onion Sauce 118
Bonbons, Black Pudding 72
Bonbons, Blue Cheese 130
Braised Lamb Shanks with Red Wine Sauce 118
Braised Red Cabbage 132, 196
Bread, Walnut 205
Brie Croutons 26
Brill Fillet with Wild Mushroom 'Vraic' 74
Brisket of Beef, (Slow-Roasted with Chasseur Sauce) 128
Brown Chicken Stock 189
Brûlée, Crème (Lemon) 142
Butter Biscuits 150, 212

C

Cabbage, Braised Red 132, 196
Cabbage, Pickled Red 122, 197
Cake, Carrot 180
Cake, Dark Chocolate Truffle 175
Cake, Fruity Teacake 176
Calvados, Baba with Apple 151
Caper Mash (Skate Wing) 76
Caper Sauce 122
Caramel 140
Carrot Cake with Orange Cream Filling 180
Casserole (Traditional Ormer) 88
Chancre Crab and Fresh Guernsey Herb Cakes
  with Chilli Dressing 90
Chancre Crab Risotto with Guernsey Herb Salad 94
Chancre Crab Sandwich 98
Chasseur Sauce 128
Cheddar, Croutes 24
Cheese, Baked 'Frie d'Or' 30
Cheesecake, Warm Gâche Melée 164
Cheesecake, Rocquette Cider 160
Cheese Sauce, Torteval Blue 50, 51, 193
Cherry Scones 179
Chicken Stock, Brown 189
Chilled Guernsey Tomato Consommé, Summer Vegetables
  and fresh Guernsey Herbs 28
Chilled Strawberry Rice Pudding with Strawberry Ice Cream 147
Chilli Dressing 90, 96
Chocolate and Chilli Ice Cream 210
Chocolate, Dark, Truffle Cake 175
Chocolate, Dark, & Orange Mousse 174
Chocolate Mousse, Dark, with Hedgerow Berries 174
Chocolate, Sponge 207
Chocolate Tart, Dark 172
Chorizo (Cuttlefish with Ink Risotto) 92
Chowder, Crab 32
Cider Cheesecake, Rocquette Cider 160
Cider, Custard 166
Cider, Jelly 160
Cider & Red Onion Soup 26
Cider & Seafood Minestrone 80
Cider Sauce, Barbequed 120
Clove Ice Cream 164, 211
C.L.T. Sandwich 98
Coffee, Sponge 207
Consommé, Chilled Tomato 28
Coulis, Red Berry 204
Crab Bisque 34
Crab Cakes 90
Crab Chowder 32
Crab Risotto 94
Crab Salad 66
Crab Sandwich 98
Cream Filling, Carrot Cake 180
Cream, Honey & Lavender 170
Crème Brûlée, Lemon 142

Tony Leck's Pavilion on a Plate

Crème Caramel	140
Crisps (Parmesan)	66
Croquette, Ham	44
Croutes, Mature Guernsey Cheddar	24
Croutons, Guernsey Brie	26
Curd, Lemon	178, 208
Custard, Floating Islands	158
Custard, Fried with Rhubarb Pannacotta	144
Custard, Rocquette Cider with	
Guernsey Gâche 'n' Butter Pudding	166
Custard, Sloe Gin	160, 209
Custard, Sultana	164, 213
Custard Tart, baked with Nutmeg	152
Cuttlefish with Ink Risotto and Chorizo	92
'Cynful Ale' 'n' Beef Pie	132
'Cynful Ale' 'n' Onion Soup	24
D	
Dark Chocolate & Chilli Ice Cream	175, 210
Dark Chocolate Mousse with Hedgerow Berries	174
Dark Chocolate & Orange Mousse	174
Dark Chocolate Tart	172
Dark Chocolate Truffle Cake	175
Dauphinoise Potatoes	114, 200
Digestive Biscuits, Oatmeal	201
Dressing (Chilli)	90, 96
Duxelle (Mushroom)	55, 128, 130
E	
Eggs; Baked with Baby Spinach	51
– Fisherman's Scotch	70
– Poached with Haddock Risotto	84
– Poached with Ham Croquette	44
– Poached Quails'	55
– Snow	158
F	
Fennel Salad	54, 64
Fig & Almond Tart with Guernsey Honey & Lavender Cream	170
Fillet, Beef Steak with Blue Cheese Bonbons,	
Mushroom Duxelle & Rocket Salad	130
Fisherman's Scotch Eggs	70
Fish in Beer Batter	100
Fish Stock	191
Floating Islands	158
'Frie d'Or' Cheese	30
Fresh Cherry Scones	179
Fresh Guernsey Chancre Crab Sandwich	98
Fresh Herm Oysters with Shallot & Red Wine Dressing	42
Freshly-picked Guernsey Crab Salad	66
Fried Custard, Rhubarb Pannacotta	144
Fruity Teacake	176
G	
Gâche, Traditional Guernsey	182
Gâche 'n' Butter Pudding with Rocquette Cider Custard	166
Gâche Melée Cheesecake, warm	164
Garlic and Mature Cheddar Croutes	24
Garlic Soup (Wild)	31
Goats' Cheese and Beetroot Risotto	56
Goats' Cheese Terrine (with Red Onion Jam)	58
Gooseberries (with Mackerel Fillets)	82
Green Pea Purée	72
Guernsey Brie Croutons	26
Guernsey Bean Jar	112
Guernsey Beef Brisket, Slow-Roasted with Chasseur sauce	128
Guernsey Beef Fillet Steak	130
Guernsey Beef 'n' 'Cynful Ale' Pie	132
Guernsey Biscuits, Tradtitional (savoury)	201
Guernsey Butter Biscuits	150, 212
Guernsey Chancre Crab Cakes	90
Guernsey Chancre Crab Risotto with Herb Salad	94
Guernsey Chancre Crab Sandwich	98
Guernsey Crab Chowder	32
Guernsey Crab Salad	66
Guernsey 'Cynful Ale' 'n' Onion Soup	24
Guernsey Gâche, Traditional	182
Guernsey Gâche 'n' Butter Pudding	
with Rocquette Cider Custard	166
Guernsey Gâche Melée with Marmalade Ice Cream	162
Guernsey Herb Salad (with Crab Risotto)	94
Guernsey Honey & Lavender Cream	170
Guernsey Honey & Oatmeal Biscuits	202
Guernsey Honey Snaps	203
Guernsey Meatballs with Tomato & Basil Sauce	136
Guernsey Ormer Casserole	88
Guernsey Scallops, seared with Black Pudding Bonbons	72
Guernsey Sea Bass Fillet	80
Guernsey Tomato & Basil Sauce	136
H	
Haddock (Poached)	84
Ham, Boiled with White Onion Sauce	118
Ham Croquette	44
Ham Hock Terrine with Parsley & Caper Pressing	38
Hazelnut, Orange & Rocket Salad	36, 56
Hedgerow Brambles, Poached Garden Pears	168
Herb Salad (with Chancre Crab Risotto)	94
Herm Oyster Ketchup	192
Herm Oysters	42, 43
Hollandaise Sauce	70, 84, 195
Honey & Lavender Cream	170
Honey & Oatmeal Biscuits	202
Honey Snaps	203
I	
Ice Cream; Basil	212
– Clove	164, 211
– Dark Chocolate & Chilli	210
– Marmalade	162
– Nutmeg	211
– Raspberry	156, 210
– Strawberry	147
– Vanilla	213
Ile flottante	158
J	
Jam, Raspberry	204
Jam, Red Onion	58, 197
Jar, Traditional Bean	112
Jelly, Rocquette Cider	160
Jelly, Strawberry	147
K	
Ketchup, Herm Island Oyster	192

Tony Leck's Pavilion on a Plate

L

Lamb Mous'SARK'a	116
Lamb Shanks with Red Wine Sauce	114
La Valée's Farm Mushroom Duxelle Tart with Poached Quails Eggs, Asparagus & Hollandaise Sauce	55
Lavender & Honey Cream	170
Leg of Mutton, Poached with Caper Sauce	122
Lemon & Vanilla Shortbread	143
Lemon Crème Brûlée	142
Lemon Curd	178, 208
Lemon, Parsley & Beetroot Butter	76
Lemon Tart, filling	154
Lemon Tart, pastry	154
Light Beer Batter	100
Lobster Salad with New Season Potatoes, Guernsey Herbs and Fennel	64
Lobster Thermidor	68
Loin of Pork with Bayeux Mustard Sauce	123

M

Mackerel Fillets with Gooseberries	82
Marmalade Ice Cream	162
Mayonnaise	194
Mayonnaise (Red Bell Pepper)	66, 98, 194
Meatballs with Tomato & Basil Sauce	136
Meadow Court Farm Beef	128, 130, 132, 136
Meringue, (Floating Islands)	158
Milk a Punch	146
Milk a Punch Pannacotta	146
Minestrone, Cider & Seafood	80
Mousse, Dark Chocolate & Orange	174
Mousse, Dark Chocolate with Hedgerow Berries	174
Mous'SARK'a of Sark Lamb	116
Mulled Spice Sugar Syrup	50, 59
Mushroom Duxelle	55, 128, 130
Mushroom, Wild, 'Vraic'	74
Mussels with Rocquette Cider, Guernsey Cream & Coriander	78
Mutton, Poached Leg with Caper Sauce	122

N

Nutmeg Ice Cream	151, 211
Nutmeg Tart, baked custard	152

O

Oatmeal Digestive Biscuits	201
Oatmeal, Guernsey Honey Biscuits	202
Oeufs à la Neige	158
Onion; Jam, Red	58, 197
– Sauce	118
– Soup, 'Cynful Ale'	24
– Soup, Red Onion & Cider	26
Orange, Beetroot & Hazelnut Salad	36, 56
Orange Cream filling, Carrot Cake	180
Orange, Dark Chocolate Mousse	174
Ormer Casserole	88
Ormers	86, 87, 88, 89
Oysters	41, 42, 43
Oyster Ketchup	192

P

Pané Mixture	70, 72, 90, 130, 144
Pannacotta, Milk a Punch	146
Pannacotta, Rhubarb with Fried Custard	144

Parmesan Crisps	66
Parsley & Beetroot Lemon Butter	76
Parsley Sauce	192
Pastry, Lemon Tart	154
Pastry, Sweet Shortcrust	170, 206
Pavilion's Traditional Guernsey Bean Jar	112
Pea Purée	72
Pears, Poached with Hedgerow Brambles	168
Pepper (Red Bell) Mayonnaise	66, 98, 194
Peppered Strawberries with Guernsey Butter Biscuits and Basil Ice Cream	150, 212
Piccalilli (with Ham Hock Terrine)	39, 195
Pickled Red Cabbage	122, 197
Pie, 'Cynful Ale' 'n' Beef	132
Pie, Potato Peel	52
Poached Free Range Eggs	44, 84
Poached Garden Pear in Mulled Spices with Torteval Blue Cheese Dip	59
Poached Garden Pears with Hedgerow Brambles	168
Poached Haddock, Baby Spinach Risotto, Hollandaise Sauce & Poached Free Range Egg	84
Poached Herm Oysters with Smoked Salmon & Cucumber	43
Poached Leg of Mutton with Caper Sauce	122
Poached Quails Eggs	55
Pork, Loin of with Bayeux Mustard Sauce	123
Pork, Slow-Roasted Belly	120
Potatoes, Dauphinoise	114, 200
Potato Peel Pie	52
Pudding, Chilled Rice	147
Pudding, Guernsey Gâche 'n' Butter with Rocquette Cider Custard	166
Pudding, Yorkshire	128, 198

Q

Quails' Eggs, Poached	55

R

Raspberry Arctic Roll with Summer Berries	156
Raspberry Ice Cream	156, 210
Raspberry Jam	204
Red Bell Pepper Mayonnaise	66, 98, 194
Red Berry Coulis	204
Red Cabbage, Braised	132, 196
Red Cabbage, Pickled	122, 197
Red Onion Jam (with Warm Goats' Cheese Terrine)	58, 197
Red Onion Soup with Rocquette Cider	26
Red Wine & Shallot Dressing	42
Red Wine Sauce	118
Rhubarb Pannacotta with Fried Custard	144
Rice Pudding, (Chilled), Strawberry	147
Risotto, Baby Spinach	84
Risotto (Crab)	94
Risotto (Cuttlefish with Ink and Chorizo)	92
Roast Brill Fillet with Wild Mushroom 'Vraic'	74
Rocket Salad with Orange & Hazelnut	36, 56
Rocquette Cider and Red Onion Soup	26
Rocquette Cider and Seafood Minestrone	80
Rocquette Cider, with Mussels	78
Rocquette Cider Cheesecake	160
Rocquette Cider Custard	166
Rocquette Cider Jelly	160
Rocquette Cider Sauce (Barbequed)	120
Roll, Arctic	156